The Death of
OMNIPOTENCE
And Birth of
AMIPOTENCE

BY THOMAS JAY OORD

SacraSage Press
SacraSagePress.com

Editorial Consultation: Devon Van Essen
Interior Design: Nicole Sturk
Cover Design: Thomas Jay Oord

Print (Hardback): 978-1-948609-90-6
Print (Paperback): 978-1-948609-91-3
Audio: 978-1-948609-93-7
Electronic: 978-1-948609-92-0

Printed in the United States of America

Library of Congress Cataloguing-in-Publication Data

The Death of Omnipotence and Birth of Amipotence / Thomas Jay Oord

TABLE OF CONTENTS

INTRODUCTION

Obituary and Birth Certificate

"*M*y *God is so big, so strong, and so mighty there's nothing that He cannot do.*"[1] These lines from a children's song give voice to what many people believe: an omnipotent God can do anything.

Contemporary Christian choruses praise an almighty God, declaring that the sovereign will cannot be frustrated. It's common for believers, enraptured in worship, to lift voices and proclaim, "*God is in control!*" The lyrics from classical music also proclaim the glory of an all-powerful deity. In his *Messiah* concerto, George Frideric Handel's oft-repeated lines ring out:

For the Lord God omnipotent reigneth,
Hallelujah! Hallelujah! Hallelujah! Hallelujah![2]

---

1. Ruth Harms Calkin, "My God is so Big" (Permission to quote granted from Nuggets of Truth Publishing, 2022).

2. Handel seems to be drawing from Revelation 19:6, which includes a word translated in Latin and in the King James Version of scripture as "omnipotent." In most contemporary biblical translations, this word, the Greek *pantocrator*, is rendered "almighty."

Omnipotence expresses in formal language the view that God can do anything. A deity with all (*omni*) power (*potens*) can apparently do anything we imagine and more. Augustine, the most influential theologian outside the Bible, makes this connection, saying the omnipotent God is "He who can do all things."[3]

In some theologies, God actually exerts all power and is the cause of everything. We might call this "theological determinism" or "monergism." In other theologies, God *could* do everything but chooses not to. God so conceived may control periodically but generally allows creatures to exert power. God willingly "withdraws" or "lets be," choosing to self-limit. Call this "voluntary divine self-limitation." In all these cases, God is essentially omnipotent.

Omnipotence is likely best known of the attributes believers ascribe to God. For many, it's a synonym for deity: "the Omnipotent." Although distinctions in meaning are possible, omnipotent is thought to be synonyms with words such as "sovereign," "all-powerful," and "almighty."[4] Only a being with unlimited power is worthy of worship.

Christian creeds refer to an all-powerful God. "I believe in God the Father Almighty, Maker of heaven and earth," begins the Apostle's Creed. The Nicene Creed starts similarly: "We believe in one God, the Father, the Almighty, Maker of heaven and earth." The Westminster Confession of Faith speaks of a "sovereign" or "almighty" God who "ordains whatsoever comes to pass."

Believers affirm various meanings of omnipotent, almighty, or all-powerful.[5] In this book, I address three meanings common among la-

---

3. Augustine, *De Trinitate, IV 20, 27* (CChr.SL), 50, 197. Despite this claim, Augustine also notes a number of things God cannot do. I address some later in this book.

4. In previous writings, I've said we could rightly call God almighty in three senses. God 1) is the mightiest, 2) exerts might upon all, and 3) is the source of might for all. Gijsbert Van Den Brink argues for "almightiness" over omnipotent in *Almighty God: A Study of the Doctrine of Divine Omnipotence* (Netherlands: Kok Pharos, 1993).

5. I agree with Alvin Plantinga when he says theists entertain various views of omnipotence. See Plantinga, "Reply to the Basingers on Divine Omnipotence," *Process Studies* 11 (1981), 28.

ity and scholars.[6] To say God is omnipotent indicates at least one of the following:

1. God exerts all power.[7]
2. God can do absolutely anything.
3. God can control others or circumstances.[8]

Some believers affirm one meaning but not all. A person might think God occasionally controls others, for instance, but reject the idea that God exerts all power whatsoever. Another may claim God can singlehandedly determine outcomes but maintain God cannot do what is illogical or self-contradictory. Yet another may say God can do absolutely anything, but God chooses not to.

It's common for believers to say God is omnipotent but appeal to mystery when vexing questions arise. "God controls all things," they say, but also insist humans have free will and God does not ordain sin. This can only be true, because "God's ways are not our ways." And "Who are we to know the mind of God?" Out comes the mystery card.

---

6. Although omnipotence is addressed in various papers, book chapters, and systematic theology sections, few monographs are devoted entirely to it. Among the books that address well the issues of omnipotence are David Basinger, *Divine Power in Process Theism* (Albany, NY: SUNY, 1988); Anna Case-Winters, *God's Power: Traditional Understandings and Contemporary Challenges* (Louisville, Ky.: Westminster/John Knox, 1990), David Ray Griffin, *God, Power, and Evil* (Washington, 1990), and Gijsbert van den Brink, *Almighty God*.

7. Some forms of Calvinism make this claim, but it also seems to be what Wolfhart Pannenberg has in mind when he says God is "the power that determines everything that exists" (*Basic Questions in Theology, Vol. 1* [London, 1970], 1).

8. Few who claim God is controlling explain what they mean. When I use "control," I mean acting as the sufficient cause of some creature, circumstance, or event. To describe such control, I use phrases like "singlehandedly decide outcomes," "unilaterally determine events," or others that depict God as the sole cause of some result. John Frame is among many who unhelpfully claim God has "control over all things." See John Frame, "The Sovereignty of God," The Gospel Coalition website (https://www.thegospelcoalition.org/essay/the-sovereignty-of-god/) Accessed 1/28/2023.

We have several reasons to ascribe omnipotence to God, say advocates of this belief. The first arises from scripture. Authors of sacred writ describe a God who does amazing things, including creating the heavens and the earth, enacting miracles, providing salvation, and promising ultimate victory over evil. While English translators typically avoid "omnipotent" when translating Hebrew and Greek biblical texts, they do refer to God as "almighty." Consequently, many people believe the Bible portrays God as all-powerful.

Given this reading of scripture, Arthur Pink expresses the import of omnipotence this way: "If God were stunted in might and had a limit to His strength, we might well despair. But seeing that He is clothed with omnipotence, no prayer is too hard for Him to answer, no need too great for Him to supply, no passion too strong for Him to subdue, no temptation too powerful for Him to deliver from, no misery too deep for him to relieve."[9] According to Pink and others, only an omnipotent God can save.

Omnipotence does not inspire hope in everyone, however. It leads some to unbelief and despair. To those who suffer intensely, a God who can eliminate pain is asleep on the job. Or this deity doesn't care enough to rescue the hurting from horrors and holocausts. Fervent prayers for healing go unanswered; cries from the abused elicit few divine rescues; children are not protected.[10] Consequently, many people have no desire to live forever with a God who allows evil now . . . if such a Being exists.

I will argue that Christian scripture does not support omnipotence. It doesn't teach that God has all power; it says there are many things God cannot do; and no passage says God controls. Biblical authors talk about

---

9. Arthur Pink, *The Attributes of God* (Grand Rapids, Mich." Baker, 2006), 67.

10. For an excellent analysis of unanswered prayer in light of God's uncontrolling love, see Mark Karris, *Divine Echoes* (Quoir: 2018). See also Bruce Epperly, *Praying with Process Theology (*River Lane, 2017); Marjorie Suchocki, *In God's Presence* (St. Louis, Mo.: Chalice, 1996).

divine action, and they consider God's power immense. But the Hebrew and Greek words translated "almighty" support neither scholarly nor popular views of omnipotence. In fact, writers of scripture acknowledge limits to divine power and point to the role creatures play in bringing about outcomes.

Omnipotence isn't born of scripture.

The second reason some consider God omnipotent pertains to philosophical theology. If God is the greatest conceivable being ("that than which nothing greater can be conceived," according to Anselm), a God who exerts all power, who can do anything, or who can control must be greater than a God without all power, who only does some things, or who cannot control. Although most scholars qualify what "do anything" means, a limited God seems less than great.

I'll argue that believing God can do anything dies the death of a thousand qualifications. Qualified omnipotence is lifeless. A look at how theologians throughout history recast and revise omnipotence reveals it was never fully alive, except as a woefully inaccurate description of divine power. Omnipotence was never alive like married bachelors and unicorns were never alive; it doesn't exist like fish who drive Corvettes don't exist. And, ironically, a word that means "without limits" requires *countless* limits.

Omnipotence must be qualified; qualified omnipotence is oxymoronic.

A third reason some affirm omnipotence arises from liturgical expressions, which lavish praise upon the divine. Liturgies chanted, sung, orated, wailed, or whispered appeal to an all-powerful deity, and they lead believers to think God has absolute power. In fact, some believers say divine power cannot be exaggerated, because God can do more than we could ask or imagine (Eph. 3:20). Let a passage from Revelation illustrate this:

> "And the four living creatures, each of them with six wings, are full of eyes all around and inside. Day and night without ceasing they sing,

Holy, holy, holy,
the Lord God the Almighty,
who was and is and is to come" (4:8).

Calling God "the Almighty" is appropriate as effusive acclaim, says this argument. We should not put words of worship through the scrutiny we require of them in biblical exegesis, systematic theology, or philosophy. Poetry expresses desires deeper than language; the mystery of omnipotence transcends feeble speech.

Worshiping God as omnipotent, however, confuses, disempowers, and harms. This injury is clearest when believers struggle to make sense of pain and suffering, whether it's suffering they experienced themselves or witnessed in family, friends, or the most vulnerable. And omnipotence directly or indirectly supports political leaders and policies, no matter how oppressive. It stands to reason that an all-powerful God installs or permits the actions of every ruler and authoritarian system.

Believers rightly wonder why an omnipotent God doesn't prevent genuine evils. The usual "answers" claim that pain is God's punishment, that God allows evil in order to educate, that God permits suffering for a greater good, and so on. But those responses do not adequately explain why an omnipotent God fails to rescue those he allegedly loves (John 3:16). Appeals to mystery fail to satisfy.

I'll argue that worship of "the Almighty" directs the faithful to think God supports whatever political leader in power or policy in place. And affirming omnipotence leads believers to think God can prevent evil singlehandedly. When oppression and unnecessary suffering occurs, however, many doubt God loves everyone all the time. This doubt is justified: we shouldn't trust an almighty God who permits evil.

Evil ends omnipotence.

Omnipotence is not born of scripture and dies the death of a thousand qualifications in philosophy. Our experience of pointless pain buries

6

omnipotence six feet under. Worshippers of various stripes—especially Christians—should stop saying God is omnipotent.

The death of omnipotence raises crucial questions. How *should* we talk about God's power? What words and ideas might replace omnipotence? How do we talk about God in ways that make sense biblically, philosophically, experientially, and theologically?

In the book's final chapter, I offer a replacement I call "amipotence." Call it a birth announcement, if you like. In previous writings, I've argued love comes first in God, and this priority matters for understanding divine power. God always acts in loving ways, but divine love never controls. Love "does not force its own way," as the Apostle Paul puts it (1 Cor. 13:5).

I go beyond what God *can't* do to explain what an amipotent God *can*. This loving God acts moment by moment, exerting causal influence throughout creation. God creates, sustains, saves, and transforms. Nothing and no one is more influential; the uncontrolling love of an amipotent God is universally active and everlasting. But the flourishing God desires requires creaturely contributions and conducive conditions in creation. A loving God needs us, because love is relational.

The death of omnipotence should be celebrated. Its demise helps us understand scripture better and overcomes conceptual conundrums that stem from thinking God exerts all power, can do absolutely anything, or can control. Burying omnipotence makes it possible to trust God as loving when we suffer. We need not sit passively on life's sidelines—like helpless damsels in distress—waiting for "the Almighty" to show up and rescue us. We have an essential role to play to promote flourishing.

Omnipotence is dead. Long live amipotence!

1

Not Born of Scripture

The words "omnipotent" and "omnipotence" are not in the Bible. But English translators render some Hebrew and Greek words as "almighty," and many readers consider "almighty" a synonym for "omnipotent." Other biblical passages seem to support the meaning of omnipotence, in the sense that God can do absolutely anything or control creation.

In this chapter, I address key biblical words and phrases pertaining to divine power: *shaddai*, *sabaoth*, and *pantokrator*.[1] Each is wrongly translated "almighty." I also address biblical passages some believe point to the meaning of omnipotence. My conclusion: the Bible does not sanction the view that God exerts all power, can do absolutely anything, or controls.

The Bible does not endorse omnipotence.

---

1. The Christian Bible has many forms, versions, and translations. I will focus primarily on the sixty-six books Protestants consider the canon, recognizing that the ancient manuscripts from which these books derive are pluriform and fluid. In fact, there is no definitive canon. On this diversity, see Brian Felushko's work and Lee Martin McDonald, *The Biblical Canon: Its Origin, Transmission, and Authority* (Grand Rapids, MI: Baker Academic, 2011).

El Shaddai

"Almighty" first appears in scripture as a translation of the Hebrew word *shaddai* (שַׁדַּי לְאֵ; *'el shaddai / šadday*). We find it in Genesis 17, when God appears to Abraham and says, "I am *el shaddai*." Many Bibles translate this phrase, "I am God Almighty." Upon self-introducing, God promises to make a covenant with Abraham and "greatly increase your numbers," provided he walks faithfully and is blameless (17:1-2).

"God Almighty" is a mistranslation of *el shaddai*.[2]

The oldest and most likely meaning of *shaddai* is "breasts."[3] The Genesis passage and others in which God is linked with *shaddai* are better translated, "I am God of breasts" or "I am the breasted God." This makes good sense given the Priestly writer's reference to Abraham's descendants; they will be born, and their mother's breast will nourish them, metaphorically speaking, so they "greatly increase."[4]

Nearly every occurrence of *shaddai* in Genesis is associated with nourishing breasts and fertility.[5] We read, for instance, that "*el shaddai* will bless you with the blessings of the heavens above, blessings of the deep

---

2. See William Albright, "The Names Shaddai and Abram," *Journal of Biblical Literature* 54 (1935): 180-93; E. L. Abel, "The Nature of the Patriarchal God 'El Sadday,'" *Numen* 20 (1973): 49-59; Lloyd Bailey, "Israelite 'El Shadday and Amorite Bl Shade," *Journal of Biblical Literature* 87 (1968): 434-38; Frank Moore Cross, "Yahweh and the God of the Patriarchs," *Harvard Theological Review* 55 (1962): 244-50; *Canaanite Myth and Hebrew Epic* (Cambridge, Mass., 1973), pp. 52-60; William G. Dever, *Does God Have a Wife? Archaeology and Folk Religion in Ancient Israel* (Grand Rapids, Mich.: Eerdmans, 2005); Jean Ouellette, "More on 'El Shadday and Bel Shade," *Journal of Biblical Literature* 88 (1969): 470-71.

3. Most scholarly assessments of the meaning of *shaddai* note diverse meanings but suggest "breast" and "mountain" as most likely. In addition to the sources cited in the footnotes below, see *NET Bible: A New Approach to Translation, Thoroughly Documented with 60,932 Notes by the Translators and Editors* (Biblical Studies Press, 2005).

4. See I. Zoller, "Il nome divino Sadday," *RSO* 13 (1931), 73-75. For why it makes sense to think of God in feminine ways, see Virginia Ramey Mollenkott, *The Divine Feminine: The Biblical Imagery of God as Female* (New York: Crossroad, 1988).

5. Klaus Koch, "Saddaj," *Vetus Testamentum* 26 (1976): 323.

lying below, blessings of breasts and womb" (Gen. 49:25). Isaac blesses Jacob saying, "*El shaddai* bless you and make you fruitful and multiply you, that you may become a community of peoples" (28:3). And "*El shaddai* appeared to me at Luz in the land of Canaan, and he blessed me, and said to me, 'I am going to make you fruitful and increase your numbers'" (Gen 48:3-4).[6] When self-introducing to Jacob, God says, "I am *el shaddai,* be fruitful and multiply" (Gen. 35:11). These examples lead David Biale to conclude that "the conception of the Hebrew God as a fertility god in general and as represented by breasts in specific has support in both biblical and extrabiblical sources."[7]

Based on the appearance of *shaddai* early in scripture and in poetic contexts, biblical scholars consider it one of the oldest names for deity.[8] In Exodus, the Lord says, "I appeared to Abraham, Isaac, and Jacob as *el shaddai*" (6:3), a passage that predates the Mosaic age.[9] The earliest biblical passages portray God as one with breasts who nourishes.

Shaddai can also refer to God as "the one of the mountain," because the Hebrew word *sadu* (mountain) is similar to *shaddai*.[10] Also, mountains

---

6. See J. Gerald Janzen's extensive analysis of *el shaddai* in relation to a personal God in *At the Scent of Water: The Ground of Hope in the Book of Job* (Grand Rapids, Mich.: Eerdmans, 2009).

7. David Biale, "The God with Breasts: El Shaddai in the Bible," *History of Religions* (1982), 252. The connection between God and breasts apparently derives from Amorite and Canaanite cultures. See also F. M. Cross, *Canaanite Myth and Hebrew Epic* (Cambridge, Mass.: Harvard University Press, 1973), 52-60.

8. Nahum M. Sarna argues that "the overwhelming appearance [of *el Shaddai*] in poetic contexts points a priori to a venerable tradition, for Hebrew poetry tends to preserve or consciously to employ early forms of speech" ("El Shaddai," *Exodus Commentary* [Jewish Publication Society, 1991], 269). See Robert Alter, *The Hebrew Bible: A Translation with Commentary*, 3 Vols. (New York: W. W. Norton & Company, 2019); G. Steins's summary, "Sadday," in *Theological Dictionary of the Old Testament*, Vol. 14 (Grand Rapids, Mich.: Eerdmans, 2004), 418-446.

9. On this, see Sarna, *Exodus Commentary*, 269. *Shaddai* is used in the blessings promised Jacob as well (Gen. 28:1-4; 35:9) and figures into the Joseph story as blessing (Gen. 49: 22-26).

10. Cross prioritizes "breast" over "mountain" as a translation of *shaddai*. "The primitive meaning [is] . . . breast. However, the secondary meaning 'mountain' developed for

are often compared to breasts.[11] The Grand Teton mountains of Wyoming, for instance, received their names from French explorers who thought they looked like breasts: *tétons*.[12]

Comparing breasts to mountains is more than visual. Mountains provide refuge, in the way mothers protect children.[13] If Abraham's descendants are to be numerous, they will need protection, and mountains represent refuge. The psalmist draws upon this protective theme: "Whoever dwells in the shelter of the Most High will rest in the shadow of *shaddai*. I will say of the Lord, 'He is my refuge and my fortress, my God, in whom I trust'" (91:1-2).

Not only is *el shaddai* mistranslated "God Almighty," but nourishment and protection do not require omnipotence. God can do these activities without possessing all power, being able to do absolutely anything, or controlling others. After all, human mothers nourish and protect without being omnipotent. *El shaddai* rendered as "God Almighty" misleads readers into thinking God is omnipotent rather than nourishing or protective.

---

transparent reasons, and early in Semitic, in view of its occurrence in both East and West Semitic." See Cross, *Canaanite Myth and Hebrew Epic*, 55.

11. Perhaps the first to see the connection between mountains and *el shaddai* is F. Deilitzsch, *Assyrisches Handwarterbuch* (Leipzig, 1896). For an argument for how "breast" became "mountain," see William Albright, "The Names Shaddai and Abram," 180-93. Manfred Weippert argues for a minority view, which says the word refers to the plains rather than mountains, "Erwagungen zur Etymologie des Gottesnamens 'El Shaddaj,'" *Zeitschrift der Deutschen Morgenlandischen Gesellschaft* 111, n.s. 36 (1961): 42-62. See also Richard Elliott Friedman, *Commentary on the Torah: With a New English Translation and the Hebrew Text* (New York: Harper One, 2003), 60; Victor P. Hamilton, "Almighty," *Theological Wordbook of the Old Testament* (Chicago: Moody Press, 1999), 907.

12. I thank Tripp Fuller for pointing out this connection.

13. See T. Nöldeke's review of F. Delitzsch, *Prolegomena eines neuen hebr. -aram. Wörterbuches zum AT* (1886), in *ZDMG* 40 (1886) 735-36; and B. Lang, *Monotheism and the Prophetic Minority. SWBA 1* (1983), 50-51. William Albright doubts this connection, however, citing "fatal phonetic obstacles," and saying, "words for 'breast' often develop the meaning 'elevation, mound, hill, mountain;' mountains shaped somewhat like breasts are frequently called 'breast, two breasts' in Arabic" (Albright, "The Names Shaddai and Abram," 183, 184).

In later books of the Bible, *shaddai* takes another meaning: destructive or warring.[14] For instance, "Cry out because the day of *Yahweh* is close, because destruction will come from *shaddai*" (Is. 13:6; cf. Joel 1:15). The psalmist sometimes depicts God as a powerful warrior: "*shaddai* scattered the kings in the land" (68:14).[15] In these instances, *shaddai* can appear "as remote, mysterious and even destructive," says Biale.[16]

The destruction motif is especially evident in Job, because *shaddai* is sometimes portrayed as causing or allowing pain, death, and destruction.[17] Job says, for instance, "*shaddai* barbs pierce me" (6:4).[18] But *shaddai* can also mean nourishment and protection in this narrative, for instance when Job recalls good days when "*shaddai* was with me" (29:5).

Job's dialogue partners—Eliphaz, Bildad, Zophar—associated *shaddai* with destruction and pain.[19] Eliphaz says, for instance, "See how happy the man is whom God reproves; do not reject the discipline of *shaddai*" (5:17). Given that Job's friends misunderstand God, however, we have reason to question the association of *shaddai* with God-ordained destruction.

---

14. *Shaddai* appears in the earlier books, then reappears in books written during or after the exile. The later occurrences point to destruction and war. See G. Steins, "Sadday," 445. Sarna argues that "the great antiquity of the name and its obsolescence in Israel in the Mosaic period explain why there are no consistent traditions as to its meaning and why the ancient versions have no uniform rendering" ("El Shaddai," *Exodus Commentary*, 269).

15. Gregory A. Boyd addresses Hebrew Bible portrayals of God as a violent warrior in *Crucifixion of the Warrior God: Interpreting the Old Testament's Violent Portrait of God in Light of the Cross,* 2 Vols. (Minneapolis, Mn.: Fortress, 2017).

16. Biale, "The God with Breasts," 245-46.

17. William Dever notes that the association of *el shaddai* with mountains was "probably conceived in pre-Israelite religion as the old Amorite-Canaanite storm god, associated with the awesome (and procreative) powers of nature." See Willam G. Dever, *Does God Have a Wife? Archaeology and Folk Religion in Ancient Israel,* 259.

18. *Shaddai* also occurs in Ruth 1:20-21 as a reference to God turning against Ruth, and scholars consider this reference as entirely poetic. On this, see Robert Alter, *The Hebrew Bible: A Translation with Commentary,* Vol. 3 (New York: W. W. Norton & Company, 2019), 628.

19. G. Steins, "Sadday," 438.

According to the story, after all, these friends do not know who God is or how God acts.

Job's fourth friend, Elihu, rightly speaks for God. But he does *not* associate *shaddai* with destruction. He uses the word like Genesis writers might: "The spirit of God formed me; the breath of *shaddai* sustains me" (33:4). The *Jewish Publication Society* translates Elihu's final reference to *shaddai* this way: "*Shaddai* is great in power and justice and abundant in righteousness; He does not torment" (37:23).

In the book of Job, the Hebrew words for God and Lord never precede *shaddai*. We find *shaddai*, but we do not find *el shaddai*. And words for God—*el, yahweh, elohim, adonai*—do not immediately precede *shaddai* in any passage that describes pain and destruction.[20] Some speculate that Old Testament writers use the word to refer to vital forces, unqualified powers, or natural factors that destroy rather than God.[21] The point is important, so I will repeat it: biblical references to *shaddai* as destructive are not directly connected with God.

These divergent meanings of *shaddai* lead us to wonder why later biblical writers use the word differently than earlier ones. Why connect God's nourishing breasts and protection with violence and destruction?

One answer says some biblical writers wanted to portray deity as both good and evil. Despite not directly connecting God with destructive *shaddai*, they wanted to say God both nourishes *and* destroys. This approach fits Isaiah's quote from the Lord: "I form light and create darkness;

---

20. Only in Genesis and Ezekiel is *Shaddai* immediately preceded by words for God. In these cases, *shaddai* is positive rather than destructive.

21. See Thorkild Jacobsen, *The Treasures of Darkness: A History of Mesopotamian Religion,* 163. Jacobsen reads the conflict in Job as a conflict between visions of God: either God is personal and concerned with individuals or God is a cosmic force. Rober Di Vito plays with a similar theory about the conflict between a parental God and an impersonal royal God in *Studies in the Third Millennium Sumerian and Akkadian Personal Names: The Designation and Conception of the Personal God* (Rome: Pontifical Biblical Institute, 1993).

I make weal and create woe; I the Lord do all these things" (45:7). It also fits stories that describe God as violent, as desiring or causing destruction.

Another possibility is that biblical writers intentionally exchanged the God of feminine breasts for a God of masculine aggression. "The transformation of *el shaddai* from a fertility god with feminine characteristics to a seemingly male god of war makes great theological and even psychological sense," argues Biale. "What better way to suppress one interpretation of a god than by substituting its opposite?"[22] This wish for a male God to sanction violence persists among readers today.[23]

There is obvious tension, if not outright contradiction, between God as a nourisher/protector and God as a destroyer/killer. For millennia, readers of the Bible have wrestled with this tension in the text. Some try to hold the opposing visions together, incoherent though the result may be. A good God, this view says, sometimes nourishes and sometimes kills.

Others opt for one image and reject the other. J. Gerald Janzen opts for God as loving nourisher, for instance, based upon the frequent recurrence of this character in the Hebrew Bible. "In a paradigm in which God is giver of conception, birth, nurture, guidance and protection and the divine source and sanction for the kin virtues of *hesed* and *rahàmim*, God is first a God of compassion."[24]

However one addresses this tension among *shaddai* meanings, my fundamental point transcends that decision: *shaddai* in scripture does not mean omnipotent and is mistranslated "almighty." Even when biblical writers portray God as destructive, *shaddai* does not mean all-powerful.

---

22. Biale, "The God with Breasts," 256.

23. One of the best arguments for nonviolence comes from Sharon L. Baker Putt, *A Nonviolent Theology of Love* (Minneapolis: Fortress, 2021).

24. Janzen, *The Scent of Water*, 36-37. For similar arguments, see Terence Fretheim's arguments in Michael J. Chan and Brent A. Strawn, eds. *What Kind of God? Collected Essays of Terence E. Fretheim* (Winona Lake, IN: Eisenbrauns, 2015); Eric A. Seibert, *Disturbing Divine Behavior* (Philadelphia: Fortress, 2009) and *The Violence of Scripture: Overcoming the Old Testament's Troubling Legacy* (Philadelphia: Fortress, 2012).

Just as breasts do not require omnipotence to nourish, warriors do not require omnipotence to destroy. A God of *shaddai* does not have all power, cannot do absolutely anything, and does not control others.

We are wise, therefore, to separate two questions. The first asks whether God, in addition to nourishing and protecting, also destroys and kills. The other asks whether *shaddai* means "omnipotent." I'll answer the first question later in this book. The second question has been my focus here, and the answer is straightforward:

> *El shaddai* does not mean "God Almighty."

Sabaoth

The second Hebrew word sometimes translated "almighty" is *sabaoth* (תוֹאָבְצ; *ṣĕbā'ôt*). This is also a mistranslation.[25]

Rather than "almighty," *sabaoth* means "forces," "armies," "hosts," "ranks," "congregation,"[26] or "council."[27] When *yahweh* or *elohim* precede it, the phrase is better translated "lord of hosts," "leader of armies," or "head of a council."[28] When *sabaoth* is not preceded by a Hebrew word for

---

25. The term is translated "Almighty" in the NIV in many instances. As examples, see 1 Sam 1:3, 11; 4:4; 15:2; 17:45; 2 Sam 5:10; 6:2, 18; 7:8, 26, 27; 1 Kgs 18:15; 19:10, 14; 2 Kgs 3:14; 17:7, 24; 19:31; Ps 24:10; 46:7, 11; 48:8; 59:5; 69:6; 80:4, 7, 14, 19; 84:1, 3, 8, 12; 89:8.

26. For the various ways *sabaoth* does not imply a military, see Cat Quine, "The Host of Heaven and the Divine Army: A Reassessment," *JBL* 138, no. 4 (2019): 741-755. For an example in which *sabaoth* refers to a council leader, see Psalm 82.

27. See Walther Eichrodt, *Theology of the Old Testament*, I (Philadelphia: Westminster, 1961); Otto Eissfeldt, "Jahwe Zebaoth," *Kleine Schriften*, 3 (Tubingen: J. C. B. Mohr Paul Siebeck, 1966); John E. Hartley, "Hosts," in *Theological Wordbook of the Old Testament* (Chicago: Moody Press, 1999), 750–751; W. H. McClellan, "Dominus Deus Sabaoth," *CBQ* 2:300–307; Patrick D. Miller, *The Divine Warrior in Early Israel* (Cambridge, Mass.: Harvard University, 1973); J. P. Ross, "Jahweh Seba'ot in Sam and Ps," *VT* 17:76–92;

28. *Sabaoth* can be preceded by many words for deity, including *Yahweh*, *Elohim*, and *Adonai*. The Septuagint occasionally uses "Lord of powers" (*kyrios (ho) theo´s tōn dyna´meōn*) for what in Hebrew would be "Lord of hosts."

God, biblical scholars *never* translate it "almighty."[29] Never. In such cases, *sabaoth* is simply translated "hosts" or something similar.

Sabaoth doesn't appear in the first books of the Bible, but elsewhere it often signifies the Lord's leadership during and after Israel's exile. The hosts being led are sometimes warriors of Israel. Other times, they are cosmic councils—other deities, planets and suns, or angels (II Kings 22:19; Deut. 4:19, 17:3; Ps. 103:20-21). Sometimes the Lord of *sabaoth* even leads hosts against Israel.

In the religion of Israel's neighbors, cosmic conflict occurred often. Warrior gods and their assemblies fought among themselves and against creatures and creation. Biblical writers worked out their views in response to these communities, sometimes integrating what they encountered, other times assimilating, and sometimes rejecting other views. "In many respects the Israelite notion of a divine assembly was quite similar to that of the surrounding cultures, particularly Canaan and Mesopotamia," says Patrick Miller, "and assuredly adapted from them."[30] Biblical scholars today explore how ancient mythologies influenced Israel's theology.

The point I'm making is that *sabaoth* never means "omnipotence" in the Bible. To lead hosts, a lord does not need to have all power, be able to do absolutely anything, or control. That *Yahweh* leads others, in fact, indicates God *doesn't* have all power. Those being led have power to cooperate or impede the Lord's plans. The fact that lords are not always

---

29. I'm grateful to Brian Felushko for his research on this important anecdote. Felushko found that *Yahweh sabaoth* (יהוה צבאות) occurs 237 times and is translated in the NRSV as "the Lord of hosts" or "O Lord of hosts." *Yahweh Elohai sabaoth* (יהוה אלהי צבאות) occurs 35 times and is translated in the NRSV as "O Lord, God of hosts" or "the Lord, the God of hosts" or "Lord, God of hosts." *Elohim sabaoth* (אלהים צבאות) occurs twice and is translated in the NRSV as "O God of hosts." *Ha-adon Yahweh sabaoth* (האדון יהוה צבאות) occurs five times, only in Isaiah, and is translated in the NRSV as "the Sovereign, the Lord of hosts." But when *sabaoth* (צבאות) is not preceded by a word for deity, which occurs five times, it is translated in the NRSV as "companies," "troops," or "armies."

30. Miller, *The Divine Warrior in Early Israel*, 59-66.

followed—whether creaturely lords or the divine Lord—suggests they have neither all power nor the ability to control.

In his summary of how *sabaoth* is used in the Bible, Patrick Miller puts the divine-creaturely interaction this way: "At the center of Israel's warfare was the unyielding conviction that victory was the result of a fusion of divine and human activity . . . it was yet possible for the people to see themselves as going to the aid of Yahweh in battle (Judg. 5:23). Yahweh fought for Israel even as Israel fought for Yahweh (Josh. 10:14; Judg.7:20-22; and so on)."[31]

Not only does the Lord of *sabaoth* lead others who exercise their own power, this warrior battles foes—divine or creaturely—who also exercise power. God cannot have *all* power if engaged in combat with opposing forces. This Lord does not control those he fights. While Israel often says their Lord is stronger than rivals, the God of *sabaoth* leads some but not all.

In sum, *sabaoth* does not mean "almighty." The God who biblical writers say leads hosts, armies, or councils acts alongside or against others with power. In fact, there is no Hebrew equivalent for the English words "God Almighty."[32] All of this leads Abraham Joshua Heschel to conclude, "the idea of divine omnipotence . . . is a non-Jewish idea."[33]

Elohim sabaoth / Yahweh sabaoth is not omnipotent.

Pantokrator in the Septuagint

Biblical writers believe God acts in powerful ways. But *shaddai* and *sabaoth* do not mean "omnipotent" and are mistranslated "almighty."

---

31. Ibid., 156.

32. For an especially insightful article on this, see Judith Krawelitzki, "God the Almighty? Observations in the Psalms," *Vetus Testamentum* (2014) 434. "God is neither explicitly characterized nor named as 'almighty' at any place in the Hebrew or Greek Psalters" (442).

33. Abraham Joshua Heschel, "Teaching Jewish Theology in the Solomon Schecter Day School," *The Synagogue School* 28 (Fall, 1969): 12.

What led to these mistranslations? The answer comes from the Septuagint (*LXX*). This ancient collection is a Greek translation of Hebrew scriptures. The Septuagint's first five books—the Pentateuch—were likely translated in the third century BCE and the remaining books in the second century. This Greek version of the Old Testament was read during Jesus' lifetime and influenced the Apostle Paul. In fact, New Testament writers quote the Septuagint more than Hebrew-language texts, and early Church Fathers used it more than Hebrew-language scriptures.

The authors of the Septuagint translate *shaddai* and *sabaoth* with the Greek word *pantokrator* (παντοκράτωρ). The prefix *panto* means "all;" the root *krater* or *krateo* has various meanings, including "hold," "seize," or "attain." For instance, God holds (*krateo*) the stars in divine hands, according to John's Revelation in the New Testament (1:16). *Pantokrator* might best be translated "all-holding" or "all-sustaining."[34]

In her explanation of how *pantokrator* emerged, biblical scholar Judith Krawelitzki says, "There is strong evidence that the [verb of] *pantokrator* has been created and established by the translators of the Septuagint." She continues, "It seems [translators] coined a new word to avoid conceptualizing *Yahweh's* power with an already known word utilized to express the power of other deities, especially Zeus's power in Greek philosophy."[35]

---

34. Ian Robert Richardson notes that "when considering God's power as providentially sustaining the universe, *kratein* was followed by the accusative case because that was used to express 'holding' rather than 'reigning.'" See Richardson, "Meister Eckhart's Parisian Question of 'Whether the omnipotence of God should be considered as potentia ordinata or potentia absoluta?'" Doctoral Dissertation (King's College London, 2002), 17. The 2nd century bishop Theophilus, for instance, says God "is called *Pantokrator* because He Himself holds (*kratei*) and embraces (*emperiechei*) all things (*ta panta*)." *Ad Autolycum* 1, 4.

35. Krawelitzki, "God the Almighty?" 442-43. Krawelitzki says that "according to the Thesaurus Linguae Graecae, less than 1% of the approximately 1400 references for [verb form of] *pantokrator* can be found in pagan literature" (cf. G. Kruse, "*Pantokrateo*" *PW* 18,3 (1949), 829-830). Although the adjective form of *pantokrator* is found only in 2 Mac. 3:22, it can be found often in Greek literature (cf. O. Montevecchi, "Pantokrator," in *Studi in onore di Aristide Calderini e Roberto Paribeni II* [Milano, 1957], 402). On the use of *pantokrator* in Greek philosophy, see H. Hommel, "Pantokrator," *Sebasmata*

Septuagint translators, says Krawelitzki, did not want to portray Israel's God as omnipotent. "It cannot be accidental that even in the Septuagint Psalter God's power is not conceptualized by the notion of omnipotence," she says. "The reluctance to name God 'the Almighty' seems to be rooted in the texts themselves, which prescind from any kind of theoretical reflection about the extent of God's power."[36] An all-holding God is not all-controlling.

The decision to represent *shaddai* and *sabaoth* as *pantokrator*, says G. Steins, "had considerable theological repercussions."[37] It not only affected the Septuagint but also affected the New Testament and later translations of both Hebrew and Greek scriptures.

Then, six centuries later (4th century AD), Jerome translated *pantokrator* as the Latin word *omnipotens* when writing the Vulgate version of the Bible. His decision to say God is *omnipotens* depends upon the Septuagint *pantokrator* and not Hebrew-language scriptures.[38] Had Jerome followed the original texts, he probably would not have used *omnipotens*, and Christians thereafter would not call God "omnipotent."

Scholars often complain that Christian theology has been unduly influenced by Greek metaphysics and Roman views of sovereignty.[39] In this

(Tübingen, 1983), 142-143; R. Feldmeier, *Nicht Übermacht noch Impotenz. Zum biblischen Ursprung des Allmachtsbekenntnisses*, eds., *Der Allmächtige. Annäherungen an ein umstrittenes Gottesprädikat* (Göttingen, 1997), 25, 30-31; M. Bachmann, *Göttliche Aumacht und theologische Vorsicht Zu Rezeption, Funktion und Konnotation des biblisch-frühchristlichen Gottesepithetons pantokrator* (*SBS* 188; Stuttgart, 2002), 147-160.

36. Krawelitzki, "God the Almighty," 443.

37. G. Steins, "Sadday," 447. On this matter, see Wilhelm Michaelis, "Κράτος (θεοκρατία), Κρατέω, Κραταιός, Κραταιόω, Κοσμοκράτωρ, Παντοκράτωρ," *Theological Dictionary of the New Testament*, Vol. 3 (Grand Rapids, Mich.: Eerdmans, 1964), 914-15.

38. Manfred Weippert, "Sadday," *Theological Lexicon of the Old Testament*, Vol. 3, Claus Westermann, ed. Mark E. Biddle, Trans. (1997), 1621.

39. Among the many, see Wolfhart Pannenberg, "The Appropriation of the Philosophical Concept of God as a Dogmatic Problem of Early Christian Theology," *Basic Questions* Vol. 2 (London 1971). Adolf Harnack is often cited as one of the first to make this charge. See his *History of Dogma*, Neil Buchanan, trans. (London: Williams and Norgate, 1897).

case, Greek beliefs likely influenced translators who chose *pantokrator*, and Roman ideas about kingly sovereignty influenced Jerome when he translated it as "omnipotent." The mistranslation, in turn, affected the writers of the creeds who called God "almighty" (*pantokrator*/*omnipotens*). The mistranslation even passed to Islam.[40] Jerome's mistaken translation from a mistaken Greek translation of Hebrew led the world's two largest religions to adopt a bogus view of divine power!

Mistaken translations of *shaddai* and *sabaoth* as *pantokrator* misrepresent God as omnipotent.

Pantokrator in the New Testament

"Almighty" appears ten times as a translation of *pantokrator* in English versions of the New Testament. Nine of those instances occur in the Book of Revelation, and one in Paul's letter to the Church in Corinth. In this section, I look at the influence of previous mistranslations.

Let me restate that *pantokrator* appears just ten times in the New Testament. This scarcity is remarkable, given that many Christians think God is omnipotent, and major creeds describe God as "almighty." The New Testament contains about 138,000 Greek words, depending on differences among early manuscripts. This means *pantokrator* occurs 0.00726% of the time. That qualifies as rare! To put it another way, New Testament writers rarely refer to God as *pantokrator*, a word often translated "almighty" in English and mistranslated from the Hebrew.

Outside Revelation, the only reference to *pantokrator* occurs in Paul's second letter to the church in Corinth. Paul writes, "As God has said: 'I will live with them and walk among them, and I will be their God, and they will be my people.' Therefore, 'Come out from them and be separate,'

See also Helmut Koester, *History, Culture, and Religion of the Hellenistic Age* in *Introduction to the New Testament*, 2nd ed. (Berlin: Walter de Gruyter, 1995).

40. M. Lidzbarski, *Ephemeris f. semitische Epigraphik*, I (1902), 258.

says the Lord. 'Touch no unclean thing, and I will receive you.' And 'I will be a Father to you, and you will be my sons and daughters, says the Lord Almighty [*pantocrator*]'" (2 Cor. 6:16b-18).

In this passage, Paul is quoting Septuagint translations of 2 Samuel 7:8, 14.[41] These verses draw from the Hebrew, *yahweh sabaoth*. We earlier saw that this phrase is rightly translated "Lord of hosts" or something similar, not "the Lord Almighty."[42] The only time the Apostle Paul—who wrote more New Testament books than anyone—refers to "*pantokrator*" is when he cites the Septuagint.[43]

In Revelation, however, *pantokrator* occurs nine times. English Bibles often render the word "almighty," as in the phrase "the Lord almighty." In most instances, *pantokrator* is a phrase of worship, with little context to discern what it means (see 1:8, 4:8, 11:17. 15:3, 16:7. 19:6, 21:22).[44] In these cases, *pantokrator* serves a liturgical function without identifying the precise connotation of the word.

John twice uses *pantokrator* to compare God to creaturely kings and emperors (16:14, 19:15). His point seems to be that God is or will be more powerful than earthly leaders. In these cases, notes Eugene Boring,

---

41. A minority of scholars believe Paul is quoting Jeremiah 31:35 here. *Yahweh sabaoth* is also used in Jeremiah, so my point stands in either case.

42. The New International Version is unique among translations when it uses "almighty" to render two New Testament words. In Romans 9:29 (Paul is citing Isaiah 1:9) and James 5:4, the NIV translates "hosts" in the Greek as "almighty." These are additional mistranslations of *sabaoth*.

43. In his analysis of Paul's reference to *pantokrator*, Wilhelm Michaelis says "it has only a loose connection with the dogmatic concept of the divine omnipotence, which is usually linked with the omnicausality of God" (Michaelis, παντοκράτωρ, *Theological Dictionary of the New Testament*, 914-15). Paul seems to switch back and forth between the Hebrew and Septuagint when citing Old Testament texts. He seems to be citing 2 Sam 7:14 here, and this passage does not include the words "says the Lord Almighty." None of the Old Testament texts Paul quotes say, "Lord Almighty." But it also possible Paul has 2 Sam 7:8 when he writes, "says the Lord Almighty," where Nathan says, "thus says *Yahweh sabaoth*." I thank Bill Yarchin for alerting me to this.

44. Michaelis notes *pantokrator* is a title found in early Jewish prayers and its liturgical use influenced the writer of Revelation (Ibid.).

"'almighty' is bound to the title 'Lord' (*kurios*), a title which properly belongs only to God but has been usurped by the emperors and used of Domitian and the other Caesars in the emperor cult."[45]

While Alexander the Great and other Hellenistic and Roman rulers *claim* to exert universal power, only God's influence is truly universal.[46] John's point is *not* that God controls, can do absolutely anything, or has all power. His point is that only a universal leader—God—exercises universal influence.

We earlier saw that *pantokrator* is a compound word, with the prefix meaning "all." In the New Testament, the verb form of the word—which refers to active power—is translated "hold," "seize," "cling," "attain," or something similar. In other words, the verb form of *krat* does not mean controlling, doing absolutely anything, or having all power.[47]

Dunamis is the Greek word in the New Testament translated "power." It occurs ten times as often as *pantokrator* and means "ability," "strength," or "influence." Biblical writers use *dunamis* to refer to the power expressed by God, Jesus, and creatures. The verb form of the word—*dunamai*—occurs about 20 times more than *pantokrator* in the New Testament. It also refers to the ability to do something.

Neither the verb nor the noun forms of *dunamis* have a prefix meaning "all" in the New Testament. If terms like *pantodunamis* or *pandunamai* were present in the Bible, we would have scriptural words that straightforwardly mean "all-powerful," "almighty," or "omnipotent." Such words are not present in scripture. Never.

---

45. M Eugene Boring, "The Theology of Revelation: 'The Lord God the Almighty Reigns,'" *Interpretation*, 259.

46. See also "Almighty," *The New Interpreter's Dictionary of the Bible*, A-C, Vol. 1 (Nashville, Tenn.: Abingdon, 2006), 105.

47. For instance, see verb forms of *krateo* in Matthew 9:25; 12:11; 18:28; 21:46; 22:6; 26:4; 26:48; 26:50; 26:55; 26:57; 28:9; Mark 1:31; 3:21; 5:41; 6:17; 7:3; 7:4; 7:8; 9:10; 9:27; 12:12; 14:1; 14:44; 14:46; 14:49; 14:5; Luke 8:54; Acts 2:24; 3:11; Colossians 2:19; 2 Thessalonians 2:15; Hebrews 4:14; 6:18; Revelation 2:1; 2:13; 2:14; 2:15; 2:25; 3:11; 7:1; 20:2.

No New Testament passages record Jesus calling God "almighty." Nor does he call God "omnipotent." Jesus doesn't use *pantokrator* or some version of *dunamis* to describe God as all-powerful. He says God is greater than himself (John 14:28), and he praises God in various ways. The word Jesus uses most often for God is "Father" or *abba*, a term of loving endearment, not overriding control.[48]

In sum, while New Testament writers describe God as having immense power, they do not use words that mean "omnipotent," "almighty," or "all-powerful." They do not use words that mean God has all power, is able to do absolutely anything, or controls. If we think Jesus knows God best, his not calling God omnipotent should influence how think about divine power.

Omnipotence isn't in the New Testament.

Is the *Meaning* of Omnipotence in Scripture?

No biblical words literally mean "omnipotent," "almighty," or "all-powerful." If portraying God as omnipotent were as important as many think, one would expect writers of sacred writ to use words that straightforwardly mean omnipotent. They don't. However, a person might claim the *meaning* of these words are present in the Bible. Perhaps biblical authors believe God is omnipotent but don't use words that explicitly say so. We need to explore this possibility.

Exerts All Power?

The claim that God literally exerts all power is the least defensible with scripture.[49] It's obviously false, given the biblical witness to creaturely

---

48. For a comparative analysis of contemporary Christologies, see Tripp Fuller, *Divine Investment* (Grasmere, Id.: SacraSage, 2019). For an analysis of Jesus' emotions, see Scott Spencer, *Passions of the Christ* (Grand Rapids, Mich.: Baker, 2021).

49. Scholars debate whether Ecclesiastes (Quohelet) identifies God as omnipotent. The book doesn't explicitly say so. But one might think life is meaningless—a common interpretation of the book's message—if an omnipotent God controls all. If all is meaningless,

actions of various kinds, especially actions God does not want. Sinful actions come to mind. In addition, *sabaoth* passages identify God working alongside or against others with power. As do numerous other Old Testament passages.

New Testament writers speak of creaturely *dunamis* alongside God's. Creatures engage, negotiate, disobey, and act variously using their powers. We are God's fellow-workers (*synergoi*), says Paul. The overwhelming biblical evidence says God is not the only one who exerts power. Creatures also act and thereby exert power.

In theological circles today, the idea that God literally exerts all power is typically linked to John Calvin. Earlier, I called the view "theological determinism" or "monergism." Whether Calvin is a full-blown theological determinist or not, other theologians are.[50] According to them, God determines all, because God is the only power.

In his essay, "God Causes All Things," the contemporary Calvinist theologian Paul Kjoss Helseth offers a word to capture theological determinism: omnicausality.[51] As the omnicause, God causes all things, because God exerts all power. Consequently, even sin, which is contrary to God's will, is caused by God. "In a wonderful and ineffable way," says

---

of course, the book of Ecclesiastes is meaningless. And we have to reason to take seriously a meaningless document. Fortunately, we don't have to think Ecclesiastes is a meaningless document nor think it portrays God as omnipotent. For writings in favor of Ecclesiastes affirming omnipotence, see C.L. Seow, *Ecclesiastes* (Yale: Yale University Press, 1997). For representatives of those who argue against omnipotence, see Jacobus Gericke, "Qohelet's Concept of Deity: A Comparative-Philosophical Perspective," *Verbum et Ecclesia* 34:1, Art. #743 (2013) and Michael V. Fox, *A Time to Tear Down & A Time to Build Up: A Rereading of Ecclesiastes* (Grand Rapids, Mich.: Eerdmans, 1999). I thank William Yarchin for alerting me to this literature.

50. Anna Case-Winters explores Calvin's view of omnipotence in *God's Power*.

51. Paul Kjoss Helseth, "God Causes All Things," in *Four Views on Divine Providence*, ed. Dennis W. Jowers (Grand Rapids, Mich.: Zondervan, 2011), 52. For a philosophical defense of full-throated theological determinism, see J. A. Crabtree, *The Most Real Being: A Biblical and Philosophical Defense of Divine Determinism* (Eugene, Or.: Wipf and Stock, 2004).

John Calvin, "nothing happens contrary to [God's] will, even that which is contrary to his will!"[52]

Some who claim that God exerts all power also say creatures exert power. In philosophical circles, this confusing view is called "compatibilism." It says that in some inexplicable way, an omnipotent God exercises all power, but creatures also exercise some.

Hermann Bavinck puts compatibilism this way: "There is no division of labor between God and his creature, but the same effect is totally the effect of the primary cause [God] as well as totally the effect of the proximate cause [creatures]."[53] Notice the words "totally" in this quote.[54] Those who adopt compatibilism assume a truly sovereign God is the total cause of all events, but creatures are also causes.

Compatibilism makes no sense to me nor to most people I know. It's nonsense, like saying, "The sandwich was made entirely by Jim, but Carol also made it." If something is done entirely by one person, another person can't contribute. Compatibilism is the attempt to join one's prior assumption that God exerts all power to the empirical observation that we and other creatures exert power. No wonder those who adopt this position call it inexplicable. It's better to say . . .

Compatibilism is a conceptual mistake.

I consider the popular phrase "God is in control" to be a form of "God exerts all power." To be in control, God must be the omnicause. But as Anna Case-Winters points out, "when God is seen as totally in control,

---

52. John Calvin, *The Secret Providence of God*, ed. Paul Helm, trans. Keith Goad (Wheaton, IL: Crossway, 2010), 81.

53. Herman Bavinck, *Reformed Dogmatics*, John Bols, ed. John Vriend, trans., Vol. 2 (Grand Rapids, Mich.: Eerdmans, 1989), 605.

54. Some versions of Thomas Aquinas's primary-secondary causal scheme assume compatibilism. For an example of a Thomist who embraces compatibilism using the primary-secondary scheme, see Michael Dodd, *Unlocking Divine Action: Contemporary Science and Thomas Aquinas* (Washington, DC: The Catholic University of America Press, 2017).

any credible concept of freedom and autonomy for human beings is relinquished and human actions lose their significance."[55] I agree.

Many say, "God is in control," but also think creatures exercise agency. They endorse compatibilism, even if they don't know the word. But this view makes no sense. God can't be in control if creatures have self-control; God can't cause all events if creatures exercise self-causation; God can't will all actions if creatures have free will.

Claiming that God exerts all power fails to describe life as we know it. It does not align with our felt experience of making free choices nor with our assumption that others choose freely. It makes God the cause of sin and evil, thereby negating our moral responsibility and undermining God's love. Believing that God exerts all power opposes scripture, because biblical writers portray humans and other creatures as exercising power.

The Bible doesn't say God exerts all power, and we should not say, "God is in control."

Able to Do Absolutely Anything?

While I find no biblical support for thinking God causes all things, some scripture passages seem to say God can do absolutely anything. These texts are rare, but this is what they say:

"Oh Lord God . . . Nothing is too hard for you" (Jer. 32:17).[56]

"I know [God] can do all things, and that no purpose of His can be thwarted" (Job 42:2).

---

55. Case-Winters, *God's Power*, 9.

56. Some translations of Genesis 18:14 have the Lord asking, "Is anything too difficult for the Lord?" This is a response to the announcement of Sarah's upcoming pregnancy. Other translations say, "Is anything too wonderful for the Lord?" Both are questions not declarations.

"With man this is impossible, but with God all things are possible" (Mt. 19:26; Mk. 14:36; cf. Lk. 1:37).

Although phrasings differ, these passages suggest God can do absolutely anything. In the next chapter, I address philosophical problems with this claim. Because of such problems, most scholars do not say, "With God all things are possible," without making numerous qualifications.

The biblical argument *against* believing God can do absolutely anything draws from other passages. These scriptures say or imply God *cannot* do some activities. Some things *are* impossible for God; God's purposes *can* be thwarted; some things *are* too hard for God. Let me cite some:

"It is impossible for God to lie" (Heb. 6:18; Tit. 1:2).

"If we are faithless, [God] remains faithful; he cannot deny himself" (2 Tim. 2:13).

"God cannot be tempted by evil and he himself tempts no one" (Jas. 1:13b).

"The Lord is the eternal God, the Creator of the ends of the earth. He cannot grow tired or weary" (Is. 40:28a).

"God cannot revoke the gifts and call" (Rom. 11:29).

"For I am the Lord, *I cannot change*" (Mal. 3:6; James 1:17).[57]

---

57. I argue that God's inability to change pertains to God's unchanging nature. Many biblical passages say or imply, however, that God's experience changes and that God repents. For my arguments, see *Open and Relational Theology: An Introduction to Life-Changing Ideas* (Grasmere, Id.: SacraSage, 2021), ch. 2.

"I cannot break my covenant nor alter the thing that is gone out of my lips" (Ps. 89:34; cf. Lev. 26:44).

"Israel, I cannot let you go. I cannot give you up" (Hos. 11:8a).

"The Lord was with the men of Judah. The men took possession of the hill country, but they were unable to drive the people from the plains, because they had iron chariots" (Judg. 1:19).[58]

"The hand of the Lord came on Elisha, and he said, 'This is what the Lord says: I will fill this valley with pools of water. For this is what the Lord says: You will see neither wind nor rain, yet this valley will be filled with water, and you, your cattle and your other animals will drink. This is an easy thing in the eyes of the Lord; he will also deliver Moab into your hands. You will overthrow every fortified city and every major town. You will cut down every good tree, stop up all the springs, and ruin every good field with stones . . .' [But] the fury against Israel was great; Israel withdrew and returned to their own land" (2 Kings 3:16-19, 27).

Some biblical passages identify certain activities as impossible given who God is. It is impossible for God to lie, for instance, because this would mean denying God's necessary characteristic of being truthful. Other biblical texts point to the limits logic places on God, an issue we explore in the next chapter. The final passages point to inabilities related to creaturely factors and actors. Each example undermines the claim that God is omnipotent in the sense of being able to do absolutely anything.

---

58. I'm grateful to Christopher Fisher for alerting me to this story. See his essay, "God is Not All-Powerful, and the Bible Tells Us So," in *Uncontrolling Love: Essays Exploring the Love of God,* L. Michaels, et. al., eds. (Grasmere, Id.: SacraSage, 2017), 167-168.

Scholars of scripture are not surprised by the examples I've listed. In fact, they could add more. Consequently, most interpret passages that say "Nothing is impossible for God" or "God can do all things" as not actually true, at least not without numerous exceptions. These statements are made in the context of specific actions God does in relation to creation; they are not broad statements about God's unlimited abilities.[59] God's abilities are not infinite.

My point: according to the Bible, God cannot do some activities.

Controls Creatures and Creation?

The final question asks whether biblical writers portray God as omnipotent if we define the word to mean "controlling creatures or creation." To control another person, creature, or situation, a controller must entirely determine the other or the outcome. To use philosophical language, to control is to act as the sole and sufficient cause. In more common language, to control is to bring about a result singlehandedly. A controlling person produces outcomes without influence from other actors or factors.

Biblical examples of God controlling would include at least two elements. First, such examples would explicitly say God acts. Second, such examples would explicitly say that *no* creaturely actors, factors, or forces exert power alongside or in addition to God. Biblical passages that explicitly describe divine omnipotence as control, therefore, would portray God as causing an outcome singlehandedly and would indicate that creaturely forces, factors, or actors did not exert causal influence.

Given these criteria, I know of no examples of omnipotent control in the *entire* Bible.

To put it more directly, I know of no scripture passages that say God controlled creatures or creation in the sense of being the only cause.

---

59. On this issue, Gijsbert van den Brink notes a difference between "abstract philosophical reasons" and "the living communication between God and man." See *Almighty God*, pp. 64-65.

Biblical writers do not describe God controlling when creating the world,[60] nor controlling when hardening Pharaoh's heart or controlling in other Old Testament stories,[61] nor controlling when Mary became pregnant, nor when God became incarnate in Jesus, nor controlling when Jesus performed miracles, nor controlling when raising Jesus from the dead,[62] nor controlling in the eschaton.[63] No biblical passage explicitly says God alone caused or will cause an outcome such that no creaturely factors, actors, or forces play a role.

The Bible does not say God controls.

Readers of scripture often *assume* God controls, however. Many come to the Bible supposing God to be omnipotent and then, imposing an idea foreign to the writers, read controlling power into the text. Even when biblical texts explicitly mention creaturely factors, many readers overlook the causal roles creatures and creation play.

The most common instances in which readers assume God is the only cause occur when biblical passages mention only God as acting and do not

---

60. For those who affirm *creatio ex nihilo*, there was nothing for God to control when initially creating. Those who reject *creation ex nihilo* usually say God worked with creaturely elements God previously created. I explain this view later in this book and in *Pluriform Love: An Open and Relational Theology of Well-Being* (Grasmere, Id.: SacraSage, 2022), ch. 8.

61. Biblical writers say God hardened Pharaoh's heart *and* Pharaoh hardened his own heart (Ex 7:13; 8:11,15,32; 9:34). I agree with Terence Fretheim that "an act of hardening does not make one totally or permanently impervious to outside influence; it does not turn the heart off and on like a faucet," and "divine hardening did not override Pharaoh's decision-making powers" (Fretheim, *Exodus: Interpretation* [Philadelphia: Westminster John Knox, 2004], 97, 99). Those who interpret "hardening" as "control" impose a view of omnipotence not required by the text.

62. On Mary's cooperation with the Spirit, Jesus' miracles, and God raising Jesus from the death—none of which control—see Thomas Jay Oord, "Essential Kenosis Christology," in *Methodist Christology: From the Wesleys to the Twenty-first Century,* Jason Vicker and Jerome Van Kuiken, eds. (Wesley's Foundery Books, 2020). Many come to these stories assuming God controls and wrongly read them as examples of omnipotence.

63. In various writings, I address God's relentless love, which does not control now or at the eschaton. See, for example, *Questions and Answers for God Can't* (Grasmere, Id.: SacraSage, 2020), ch. 7. For an eschatology based on the renewal of the heavens and earth, see Richard Middleton, *A New Heaven and a New Earth* (Grand Rapids, Mich.: Eerdmans, 2014).

mention creaturely factors. A biblical passage might say, "God did X." In this case, many readers jump to the conclusion that God acted alone and controlled creatures or creation. Because the text does not mention creaturely causes, many *assume* God brought about an outcome singlehandedly.

Compare "God did x" with how we talk about everyday events. We might say, for instance, LeBron James won the basketball game. This can be true and yet also true that other actors and factors—his teammates, the coach who drew up the plays, opposing players, his own physical health, the fans, the referees, and so forth—played causal roles in the victory. Although we say, "LeBron won the game," it wasn't LeBron acting alone.

Or we might say, "Graysen rode her bike to the store." This may sound as though *only* Graysen brought about the result. The truth is that many forces, factors, and actors were necessary, including a functioning bicycle, cooperative humans and perhaps dogs who could have impeded her, the force of gravity, healthy legs capable of responding to Graysen's desires, decent weather, and much more. "Graysen rode her bike to the store" does not mean Graysen alone produced the outcome.

"But LeBron and Graysen aren't the omnipotent God of the universe," someone might respond. This is true. But notice that "omnipotent" is an assumption one brings to reflection about God. While we all have assumptions, the Bible doesn't explicitly support the assumption that God is omnipotent in the sense of singlehandedly bringing about results.

Every situation or event in life involves multiple forces, factors, and actors. No one brings about outcomes unilaterally. Unfortunately, many readers of scripture set aside what they know from experience and assume God acts as a solitary cause. But I know of no biblical passage that says God alone brought about an outcome *and* no creaturely actors or factors were involved. None.

Several biblical texts say, for instance, "God brought Israel out of Egypt." Readers might assume the texts mean that God acted alone in delivering Israel. This assumption ignores the creaturely factors, actors, and forces that played essential roles in Israel's release from captivity, even though these creaturely causes are explicitly identified in the biblical accounts.

Take as another example the first verses of Genesis (1:1-2). The NIV interprets them this way: "In the beginning God created the heavens and the earth. Now the earth was formless and empty, darkness was over the surface of the deep, and the Spirit of God was hovering over the waters." The updated version of the NRSV renders the same passage this way: "When God began to create the heavens and the earth, the earth was complete chaos, and darkness covered the face of the deep, while a wind from God swept over the face of the waters."

Both versions say God created. But neither says God created *alone*. The text does *not* say, "An omnipotent God singlehandedly created everything, and no creaturely factors or actors contributed." In fact, the Genesis writers identify creaturely forces and factors present (e.g., earth, deep, waters, chaos).[64] God creates alongside creation.

Terence Fretheim notes the significance of multiple actors and factors in the biblical texts. "The creation accounts demonstrate that God chooses not to act alone in bringing the creation into being," he says. "While God is certainly the initiator and primary actor in creation, God certainly involves both the human and the nonhuman in the continuing process

---

64. This list of biblical scholars who say Genesis does not teach creation from nothing is long. For examples, see Terence E. Fretheim, *God and World in the Old Testament: A Relational Theology of Creation* (Nashville: Abingdon Press, 2005), 5; Rolf P. Knierim, *Task of Old Testament Theology* (Grand Rapids, Mich.: Eerdmans, 1995), 210; Levenson, *Creation and the Persistence of Evil*; Shalom M. Paul, "Creation and Cosmogony: In the Bible," *Encyclopedia Judaica* (Jerusalem: Keter, 1972), 5:1059-63; Mark S. Smith, *The Priestly Vision of Genesis 1* (Philadelphia: Fortress, 2010), 50; Bruce K. Waltke, *Creation and Chaos* (Portland, Or.: Western Conservative Baptist Seminary, 1974); John H. Walton, *The Lost World of Genesis One* (Downers Grove, IL: IVP, 2009), 42; Claus Westermann, *Genesis 1-11*, John J. Scullion, trans. (London: SPCK, 1994), 110; Frances Young, "Creatio Ex Nihilo: A Context for the Emergence of Christian Doctrine of Creation," *Scottish Journal of Theology* 44 (1991): 139-51.

of creation."[65] God's creating is not solitary: "God works creatively with already existing realities to bring about newness."[66] Fretheim offers this hermeneutical principle: "God and creation must be considered together, because again and again the texts keep them together."[67]

Does Mighty Deeds?

I've mentioned God's creating the world and delivering Israel alongside creaturely actors, factors, and forces. Biblical scholars identify other events they call the "mighty deeds" of God. Many readers assume those mighty acts could occur only if an omnipotent God singlehandedly accomplished them. Mighty deeds require divine control, this argument says.

Gijsbert van den Brink appeals to this logic: "God's omnipotence appears from His *actions*."[68] Assuming God has "unlimited power or ability to bring things about by acting in the world," van den Brink says the Bible supports omnipotence. "From their experience of God's mighty acts, people [in scripture] came to the conclusion that nothing could be impossible for this God."[69] In short, "the best reason to believe that God is omnipotent is because He has revealed Himself as such, and that the way in which His omnipotence should be interpreted is determined by this revelation."[70]

I disagree. Biblical writers often describe God as powerful. "Great is the Lord and mighty in power," says the Psalmist, for instance (147:5). And I affirm the mighty deeds of God in scripture. But God can be powerful and do mighty deeds without being omnipotent. In the final chapter, I offer a theology of God's immense power that accounts for the mighty deeds but denies God is all-powerful. Here, I offer five responses to the

---

65. Fretheim, *God and the World in the Old Testament*, 48.

66. Ibid., 5.

67. Ibid., xvi.

68. Van den Brink, *Almighty God*, 166. The emphasis on "actions" is the author's.

69. Ibid., 176, 177.

70. Ibid, 5.

idea God must control creatures or creation—in the sense of singlehandedly bringing about results—to do mighty deeds.

First, biblical writers do not explicitly say God acted alone to bring about the mighty deeds in salvation history. The text doesn't plainly say God is omnipotent in the sense of controlling others. This is an assumption many bring to the Bible, not a conclusion it requires. For more on this, see my arguments above.

Second, it is possible (and I will argue later) that God did these mighty deeds—including miracles—alongside and with the cooperation of creation rather than by omnipotent control. Perhaps God *requires* creaturely cooperation or the conducive conditions of creation. In other words, God can do mighty deeds *alongside* cooperating creatures and conducive conditions, so the "mighty acts of God" don't require God to singlehandedly determine outcomes.

Judith Krawelitzki joins Fretheim and other biblical scholars in noting that Old Testament writers repeatedly describe God working *with* creatures. "*Yahweh* is my strength," says Krawelitzki, "because he enables my rescue by letting me participate in his power." God's "mighty deeds are not demonstrations of [God's] power for his own sake," she continues. "Rather, they are salvific and rescuing deeds. God bestows his power in creation and history in order that his people can participate in his power by his deeds."[71]

Third, although many scholars deny God controls humans, they assume God must have absolute control when it comes to less complex creatures and inanimate matter. Scripture does not require this hard distinction, however, between God's activity alongside complex humans and

---

71. See Krawelitzki, "God the Almighty?" 441-42. Walter Brueggeman argues similarly: "the theological substance of Hebrew Scripture is essentially a theological process of vexed, open-ended interaction and dialogue between the Holy One and all those other than the Holy One." "Biblical Theology Appropriately Postmodern," in *Jews, Christians, and the Theology of the Hebrew Scriptures*, Alis Ogden Bellis and Joel S. Kaminsky, eds. (Society of Biblical Literature, 200), 100.

less complex creatures. In fact, the distinction is based on metaphysical assumptions about creation as dead, empty, or mindless. By contrast, biblical writers often describe creation—animals, plants, elements—as alive, enchanted, or spirited. Perhaps God works alongside and with even the simplest of entities and elements.

Fourth, and especially importantly, biblical writers describe many times when God does *not* perform mighty deeds. God sometimes fails to rescue Israel, for instance, or to deliver people from suffering and death. While in exile, in captivity, or under foreign rule, the people called for divine help. God did not always rescue. Some wondered whether God had abandoned them; others wondered whether God was punishing them. The writers of scripture often lament when God *fails* to liberate, and this failure is not rare.

A robust description of divine power must account for what a loving God does and doesn't do. It must explain the mighty acts of salvation history *and* the history of suffering and evil. It must explain why God sometimes rescues and sometimes can't.

Finally, most Christians consider Jesus Christ the clearest revelation of God. In the witness of Jesus, we find a God who does not dominate (*astheneias*). God is made known to us in the one whose crucifixion on a cross, according to the Apostle Paul, demonstrates divine weakness (1 Cor. 1; 2 Cor. 13:4). Jesus' servant-like life reveals God as self-giving (*kenosis*) rather than controlling (Phil. 2). The life, death, and resurrection of this humble Nazarene display strength and weakness but not control.[72] The Christological witness ought to influence our view of divine power.

---

72. John D. Caputo explores this theme in *The Weakness of God: A Theology of the Event* (Bloomington, Ind.: Indiana University Press, 2006). We find it also in Martin Luther's theology of the cross. See Alister McGrath, *Luther's Theology of the Cross* (London: Blackwell, 1990) and Paul Fiddes, *The Creative Suffering of God* (Oxford: Clarendon, 1992). Daniel L. Migliore, *The Power of God and the gods of Power* (Louisville, Kent.: Westminster/John Knox, 2008), 41.

In sum, the Bible fails to support omnipotence understood as control. Given widespread biblical references to God working alongside creatures and creation, we have grounds to speculate God that does mighty acts without coercing. Accounting for God's might and weakness—the mixed witness in scripture and mixed witness today—is required to account for divine power. "If we attend closely to its story," says Daniel Migliore, "the Bible subverts and transforms our conventional understandings of power."[73]

Conclusion

The Bible does not support omnipotence.

The Hebrew words *shaddai* and *sabaoth* are mistranslated as *omnipotens* in Latin and "almighty" in English. The words actually mean "breasts," "mountains," "hosts," "armies," or something similar. And the context in which these words appear does not lend support to their being translated as "almighty."

Greek writers of the Septuagint (*LXX*) mistranslated these words as *pantokrator*, and this led to immense confusion and error. *Pantokrator* does not mean "almighty" or "omnipotent," in the sense of God exerting all power, controlling others, or being able to do absolutely anything. It is better translated as "all-holding."

New Testament writers do not consider God omnipotent. They rarely use the word *pantokrator* and never *dunamis* in ways that mean God is all-powerful. The Apostle Paul only uses *pantokrator* once, and that's when he's quoting the Septuagint. Jesus never says God is almighty. The New Testament does not portray God as omnipotent.

---

73. Daniel L. Migliore, *The Power of God and the gods of Power* (Louisville, Kent.: Westminster/John Knox, 2008), 41.

The meaning of omnipotence is not in scripture. If the word means "exerts all power," the Bible repeatedly describes creatures exerting power, often in opposition to what God wants. If omnipotence means "able to do anything," numerous biblical passages and stories describe activities God cannot do. If omnipotence means "controls creatures or creation," no biblical passage explicitly claims God controls. No passage says God brings about results singlehandedly, such that no creaturely actors, factors, or forces were involved. As described in the Bible, God is strong and weak; God sometimes does mighty acts and other times fails.

Omnipotence is *not* born of scripture.

2

Death by a Thousand Qualifications

I began by citing a children's song that says God is so strong, so big, and so mighty there's nothing that He cannot do. This song and many like it ascribe omnipotence to God. In the last chapter, I reported that Hebrew and Greek words in scripture are mistranslated "almighty." The meanings of omnipotence are not in holy writ; biblical writers identify activities God cannot do; scripture does not say God controls. The Bible does not support omnipotence.

In this chapter, I address omnipotence from philosophical perspectives. I first pondered the possibility that God could not do some activities in a philosophy class. Someone asked, "Can God make a rock so big even God can't lift it?"[1] This question sent me into an intellectual tailspin: What was the proper response? I had not considered the possibility that God's abilities may be limited. I was flummoxed.

---

1. For sophisticated presentations of this question and its implications, see George Mavrodes, "Necessity, Possibility, and the Stone which Cannot be Moved," *Faith and Philosophy* 2 (1985), 265-71; Savage, C. Wade. "The Paradox of the Stone." *Philosophical Review*, Vol. 76, No. 1 (January 1967), 74–79.

Over time, I discovered the rock question was one of many puzzles troubling people who take rationality seriously. Thomas Aquinas admits to being confused, for instance, about "the precise meaning of the word 'all' when we say that God can do all things." Consequently, he says, it's "difficult to explain in what omnipotence precisely consists."[2] In response to various concerns, nearly every serious theologian says God cannot do some things. God can't.

People wanting clarity will qualify omnipotence in countless ways. In fact, the number and types of qualifications make it nonsensical to say, "God is omnipotent." Ironically, to many people omnipotence means "without qualification." To qualify repeatedly a word that means "without qualification" is commit dictiocide: to kill the word.

Omnipotence dies the death of a thousand qualifications.

To Qualify a Claim

Before looking at the ways philosophers and theologians qualify omnipotence, I want to make clear what I mean by "qualify." To qualify a concept or claim is to note its limits and exceptions. A person qualifies by adding provisos, conditions, modifications, stipulations, or exemptions.

For instance, someone might say, "New York is the greatest city in the world . . . but Paris is better in the spring." In this statement, the person qualifies the claim New York is greatest. Someone might say, "Every year has 365 days . . . except when it's a leap year." That's an exception. Not *every* year has 365 days. Or "She's the nicest person you'll ever meet . . . after she's had a cup of coffee." In this example, the woman's niceness is conditional. Each qualified claim is stipulated, limited, or excepted.

---

2. Thomas Aquinas, *Summa Theologica,* I (Westminster, Md: Christian Classics, 1981), 1a, Q. 25, A. 3.

Superlative words are especially prone to qualification. "I see that guy *everywhere*" is an obvious exaggeration, for instance, and we assume qualifications. He's not omnipresent. "Ask Cheryl; she knows everything" is an overstatement needing limits. Cheryl isn't omniscient.

God has superlative attributes. According to most theologians, God is all-knowing (omniscient), all-loving (omnibenevolent), present to all creation (omnipresent), living in all times (everlasting), and so on. In this chapter, I argue that the superlative "God is all-powerful" (omnipotent) requires excessive qualifications. In fact, the number and nature of provisos disqualify omnipotence as an appropriate description of divine power.

God Cannot Do What is Contradictory

Earlier, I noted a question posed in philosophy class: Can God make a rock so big God can't lift it? The standard answer among philosophers says God *cannot* make such a rock.[3] Doing so involves an ontological contradiction, so it's impossible. Such contradictions limit everyone, including God, because they are inherently undoable.[4]

We could add similar activities no one can do. The popular philosopher Homer Simpson asked about one such activity: "Could Jesus microwave a burrito so hot that he himself could not eat it?" Because we're addressing God's power, I'll pose these ontological contradictions as divine limits. Here are a few:

---

3. For a sophisticated exploration of this issue, see Savage, C. Wade. "The Paradox of the Stone," *Philosophical Review*, Vol. 76, No. 1 (Jan. 1967), pp. 74–79. For an unsophisticated exploration, see Donald Bloesch, who says "The God of the Bible is not bound by the rigors of human logic" (*God the Almighty* [Downers Grove, Ill.: IVP, 1995], 58). The best representative of the minority opinion on this is Rene Descartes. See his *Philosophical Letters*, A Kenny, trans. (Minneapolis: University of Minnesota Press, 1970).

4. The literature exploring contradictions to omnipotence is immense. For a recent discussion, see Michael Wreen, "The Contradiction Approach to Solving Problems about Omnipotence," *International Journal for Philosophy of Religion and Philosophical Theology* (2022): 259-70.

God cannot make a mountain so high God cannot climb it.

God cannot make a creature so small God cannot find it.

God cannot make a river so wide God cannot cross it.

God cannot create a jail so secure God cannot escape it.

I could add a thousand examples of things God cannot do because they are ontologically impossible. Such examples do not surprise most philosophically minded people. And even the most conservative theologians admit limits on divine omnipotence and qualify what they mean by the word.[5]

Let perhaps the most influential philosophical theologian in Christian history—Thomas Aquinas—explain this. "Whatever implies contradiction does not come within the scope of divine omnipotence," he says, "because it cannot have the aspect of possibility." So "whatever implies a contradiction cannot be [possible with God], because no intellect can possibly conceive such a thing."[6]

In addition to ontological limits, most scholars qualify omnipotence by saying God cannot do the mathematically impossible. I could easily list a thousand mathematical equations God cannot make true. Here are a few:

God cannot make 2+2=1.

God cannot make 24 ÷ 12 = 47791.

---

5. As an example of a conservative theologian who qualifies divine omnipotence, see Stephen Charnock, *The Existence and Attributes of God,* 2 vols. (Grand Rapids, Mich.: Baker Book, reprint 1996 [1853]).

6. Thomas Aquinas, *Summa Theologica,* 1a, Q. 25, A. 3, Respondeo.

God cannot make 3 x 4 = 110,093.

God cannot add two integers and get a fraction.

Closely related to the laws of mathematics are the laws of geometry. An omnipotent God cannot break these laws, which means they deny additional activities to God. To put it another way, the principles of geometry point to things God cannot do. Here are a few examples, although thousands could be added:

God cannot make a round square.

God cannot create a triangle whose angles do not add up to 180°.

God cannot make the circumference of a circle 5nr.

God cannot make the area of a rectangle base x height x 67.

Related to the laws of ontology, mathematics, and geometry are the laws of logic. Most theologians admit that God cannot break these laws. Again, thousands of examples could be listed. Here are a few, beginning with the fundamental law of noncontradiction:

God cannot make something both "A" and "Not A."

God cannot make a married bachelor.

God cannot make a hornless unicorn.

God cannot make a living cadaver.

Each example identifies limits to what God can do based on various contradictions. Nick Trakakis summarizes my point when he says, "No matter how much controversy and debate may currently surround the extraordinary attribute of divine omnipotence, there is a virtually complete consensus amongst philosophers and theologians that Aquinas is correct in saying that 'anything that implies a contradiction does not fall under God's omnipotence.'"[7]

God cannot do activities that entail ontological, mathematical, geometric, or logical contradictions.

God Cannot Deny God's Nature

In addition to thousands of contradictions like those I listed above, additional qualifications to divine power are required. Some pertain to who God is, or what most call "the divine nature."[8]

Thomas Aquinas is not exactly right to say, "God can do all things that are possible; and for this reason He is said to be omnipotent."[9] After all, many actions are possible for creatures but impossible for God. So God can't do *all* things possible.[10] In the last chapter, for instance, we noted that biblical writers say it's impossible for God to lie (Heb. 6:18; Tit. 1:2). In this case, you and I can do something God cannot.

We need to explore qualifications to omnipotence that arise from God's nature. For various reasons, these qualifications are important. Most, if not

---

7. Nick Trakakis, "An epistemically distant God? A critique of John Hick's response to the problem of divine hiddenness," *Heythrop Journal* 48 (2007), 55.

8. Among important books exploring the meaning of God's nature, see Alvin Plantinga, *Does God Have a Nature?* (Milwaukee, 1980).

9. Thomas Aquinas, Summa Theologica, 1a, Q. 25, A. 3. Given what Aquinas says in other discussions, I suspect he'd agree with my criticism. He should have said, "'God can do all things' is rightly understood to mean that God can do all things that are possible for God." But even adding the qualification "for God" is unhelpful, because it begs the question about the nature of God and how that nature limits divine abilities.

10. This undermines Aquinas' recommendation that it "is better to say that such things cannot be done, than that God cannot do them." (Ibid.) Many things *can* be done, just not by God.

all, fall under the general biblical claim that "God cannot deny himself" (2 Tim. 2:13). These are impossibilities for God, given who God is.

To begin exploring these activities, I turn to Augustine. He offers the following qualifications to divine power: "I can tell you the sort of things [God] could not do," he writes. "[God] cannot die, He cannot sin, He cannot lie, He cannot be deceived. Such things He cannot."[11] Let me list these four like this:

God cannot die.

God cannot sin.

God cannot lie.

God cannot be deceived.

Other theologians add qualifications.[12] Many arise from the superlative attributes I mentioned earlier. For instance, a God who exists necessarily cannot decide to stop existing. The God who is present to all cannot be absent someplace. An omniscient God cannot be ignorant of some fact. A God who by nature loves everyone and everything cannot be unloving toward someone or something.[13] We might list these qualifications this way:

---

11. Augustine, *Sermo de symbolo ad catechumenos* 2 (CChr.SL 46, 185-6, PL), 40. Augustine strangely adds that if God could do such activities, "He would not be omnipotent." This makes little sense, however. Imagine saying that Tom can't speak all languages because if he could, he would not be omnipotent.

12. Stephen Charnock offers a good discussion of things God cannot do. See *The Existence and Attributes of God*, 1-40.

13. Wes Morriston ably defends the claim that a morally perfect God cannot be omnipotent. See Morriston, "Omnipotence and necessary moral perfection: are they compatible?" *Religious Studies* 37 (2001), 143–160.

God cannot decide to stop existing.

God cannot be omnipresent and absent somewhere.

God cannot be omniscient and ignorant of some fact.

God cannot be all-loving but fail to love someone.

The question of the priority of choice or love leads some theologians to say God can't choose not to love. God *must* love. Jacob Arminius makes the point when he argues "God is not freely good; that is, he is not good by the mode of liberty, but by that of natural necessity." For "if God be freely good," Arminius continues, "he can be or can be made not good." In fact, Arminius considered blasphemous the idea God chooses to love.[14] Divine omnipotence must be qualified to say God cannot choose evil.

Believers may think these qualifications inconsequential. "Isn't it true by definition that God always exists, is omnipresent, and loves everyone?" they might ask. "Why should anyone think of these as limits to divine power?"

If we compare these qualifications with scripture, however, we'll see why they matter. In fact, affirming each one forces us to make choices when interpreting biblical passages that conflict. Do we accept as true passages that say God never harms, for instance, or those that say God sometimes harms? Do we accept passages that say God loves everyone or those that say God only loves some? Do we accept passages that say God sometimes abandons us or those that say God never leaves us? And so on.

Suppose we say God *can* choose to stop loving everyone. Or God *can* choose to be absent from some situation. These choices commit us to other qualifications. The God who can choose to stop loving or not be

---

14. Jacob Arminius, "It is the Summit of Blasphemy to Say God is Freely Good," in *The Works of Jacob Arminius*, James Nichols, trans. (1828; repr. Grand Rapids, Mich.: Baker, 1991), 2:33-34.

present is unable necessarily to love all and necessarily to be present to all. When it comes to God's nature, in other words, we can't avoid qualifying omnipotence.

Another set of qualifications to divine abilities is necessary to account for God's uniqueness. Most theologians are monotheists and believe God has no divine colleagues. This means, according to many, God is unable to create an equal or superior deity. Peter of Lombard identifies this issue when he says, "God could not generate someone better than himself, for there is nothing better than God."[15] We can identify a myriad of ways God cannot create someone better.

God cannot create someone smarter than God.

God cannot create someone stronger than God.

God cannot create someone more loving than God.

God cannot create an infinite divine being.

Theologians differ among themselves on some qualifications of omnipotence, of course. What is often called "classical theism" adds modifications that I would not.[16] For instance, classical theism makes these qualifications to omnipotence:

God cannot decide to change, because God is immutable.

God cannot be affected by creatures, because God is impassible.

---

15. Peter Lombard, I *Sentences*, d. 44, c. 1, 1 (188).

16. R.T. Mullins offers a concise and well-defended explanation of classical theism in "Classical Theism," *T & T Clark Handbook of Analytic Theology*, James M. Arcadi and James T. Turner, Jr., eds. (London: Bloomsbury, 2021). See my exploration of classical theism in relation to love in *Pluriform Love*, "Classical Theism and *Because of* Love," ch. 6.

God cannot experience the flow of time, because God is timeless.

God cannot feel emotion in response to creatures, because God has no such emotions.

The limits to omnipotence I've noted appeal to principles to which even God seems subject. "Where are these principles?" we might ask. "Who created them?" A common answer and one I accept says no one—not even God—created them.[17] These principles—often called "Platonic forms"—are everlastingly part of God's uncreated nature. For God to deny them, therefore, God would have to deny Godself . . . which God cannot do.[18]

Many qualifications I've noted fall under the broad claim that God did not create Godself. This means, in part, that God did not and cannot create God's own nature. This inability is widely assumed and affirmed among theistic scholars.[19] Or as Charles Taliaferro puts it, "the state of affairs of *God's being God* is not something God could have brought about or altered."[20] Let me list it simply:

God cannot create God's nature.

---

17. The vast majority of theologians and theistic philosophers think God did not create possibilities, eternal truths, numbers, and abstracta. They are part of God's nature or reside in the divine mind. Rene Descartes is among those in the minority view (See Descartes, "Letters to Mersenne, Meslend, and More," in *Philosophical Letters*. I recommend Gijsbert van den Brink's explanation of this issue and the few contemporary advocates of Descartes' position. See Van den Brink, *Almighty God*, ch. 2.

18. See my discussion of this issue in *The Uncontrolling Love of God: An Open and Relational Account of Providence* (Grand Rapids, MI: InterVarsity, 2015), ch. 2.

19. Arminius offers a list of things God cannot do in "Twenty-Five Public Disputations," *The Works of James Arminius*, 135.

20. Charles Taliaferro, *A Contemporary Philosophy of Religion* (Oxford: Blackwell, 1998), 71.

One issue that deserves special attention is God's relation with creation. An interesting set of qualifications to omnipotence emerge when we consider it. Because it leads to odd conclusions, I devote the next section to God's relationality with creatures.

God Cannot Both Exert All Power and Relate with Creatures

We earlier saw that some understand "omnipotent" to mean God exerts all power. This seems to be what Wolfhart Pannenberg means when he says, "The word 'God' is used meaningfully only if one means by it the power that determines everything that exists."[21]

In various writings, Charles Hartshorne points out problems that come from saying God exerts all power. I want to address two.

To Exist is to Exert Power

The first problem Hartshorne identifies arises from what it means to exist. He follows in the tradition of Plato and Alfred North Whitehead when he says that to exist is to exert power.[22] All existing beings and entities exert a measure of influence, including people, planets, cats, volcanoes, worms, cells, and quarks. The degrees of power that creatures and objects exert vary depending on their size, complexity, relationships, composition, and so on. For instance, a human is more powerful than a ladybug. A ladybug is more powerful than a cell. But everything actual exerts power.

This claim fits existence as we know it. If we accept it as true, however, a problem emerges. If God exerts *all* power whatsoever, nothing else exerts power. Nothing. This conclusion leaves us with two options: 1) we and other creatures do not exist, or 2) we and other creatures *are* God.

---

21. Pannenberg, *Basic Questions in Theology, Vol. 1*, 1.

22. S. Lukes agrees with Hartshorne. See *Power: A Radical View* (London, 1974).

The first cannot possibly be true. I'm aware that I'm typing this sentence, for instance. I exist. And you are reading this sentence. You exist. Even solipsists admit to their own existence.[23]

If the second option is true, I am God. And so are you. If we're both God, pantheism is true, and there is no distinction between Creator and creatures. Along with most theists, I don't think God and humans are identical. My wife also denies I'm God!

Those who claim God exerts all power engage in self-refuting action. Unless they also claim to be God, the very act of claiming this is an exertion of their own power. God can't exert *all* power and we exert some.

Fortunately, few people think God exerts all power. Many say an omnipotent God *essentially* has all power but voluntarily shares some with creatures.[24] In this view, God creates and sustains creatures moment by moment but enables them to exert power. This makes possible give-and-receive relationships between Creator and creatures too. The typical version of this view says God occasionally controls creatures by single-handedly causing outcomes. But usually, God does not; creatures exert the power God voluntarily gives them.

Hartshorne's criticism of omnipotence also affects this view. An omnipotent God who sometimes unilaterally determines others as their sufficient cause does not *always* give power. Or this God momentarily withdraws or overrides the power given. The common claim that miracles are "supernatural" assumes occasional divine control in this sense.[25]

If Hartshorne is right that to exist, creatures must exert power, God's momentary decision *not* to give power or override the power given leads

---

23. Solipsism is the philosophy that nothing exists outside one's own experience.

24. An especially good collection of writings on this issue is *The Power of God: Readings on Omnipotence and Evil*, Linwood Urban and Douglass Walton eds. (Oxford: Oxford University Press, 1978).

25. David Ray Griffin offers one of the better arguments against supernaturalism understood as divine control of creation. See *Reenchantment without Supernaturalism: A Process Philosophy of Religion* (Ithaca, NY: Cornell University Press, 2001).

to odd conclusions. In the moment a creature doesn't have power, it must stop existing. Poof! It's gone . . . at least temporarily. If miracles require momentary supernatural control, the creatures involved disappear into nothingness. Odd![26]

One might respond, "No, controlled creatures continue to exist. God only momentarily suspends their power. Miracles occur when divine power is supernaturally expressed in or through creatures or creation." Or as Gijsbert van den Brink puts it, "God is able to remain the fully sovereign Lord of history, since He has the power to suspend our freedom as often as He wishes." In this, says van den Brink, God's intervention is occasional, "restoring our freedom afterwards."[27]

This response leads to another odd conclusion. If creatures, even for a moment, have no power of their own but only divine power expressed through them, they momentarily must become divine. If all of their power is divine, they're God. When divine power entirely replaces creaturely power—even for a moment—the Creator-creature distinction evaporates. Controlled creatures are not God's metaphorical hands and feet; they're literally divine. Odd!

Power is Social

The second claim Hartshorne makes about omnipotence relates to the first. He says power is fundamentally social. "Power must be exercised upon something," he says.[28] Power does not exist in absolute isolation.[29] If

---

26. Charles Hartshorne agrees and says omnipotence "condemns God to a dead world, probably indistinguishable from no world at all" (*Omnipotence and Other Theological Mistakes* [Albany, NY: State University of New York Press, 1984], 18).

27. Gijsbert van den Brink, *Almighty God*, 224.

28. *Hartshorne, Man's Vision of God, 89.*

29. See Simon Kittle's work on this, including "The Incompatibility of Universal, Determinate Divine Causation with Human Free Will," In Vicens, L. and Furlong, P. *Theological Determinism: New Perspectives* (Cambridge University Press, 2022), 100-118.

this is true, no one—including God—can have a monopoly on power.[30] And solipsism is false.

Given that any exercise of power occurs in relation to others, God must be "one power among others," as Hartshorne says, "not the only power."[31] This way of thinking fits well with our experience and the biblical witness.[32] And it's necessary for drawing analogies between divine and creaturely power.

If all power is social, however, more odd implications emerge for those who affirm omnipotence. For instance, if power is social but God once existed without creaturely others, this God without creation had no power. Odd. And if creating requires power, a solitary God would be powerless to create. So . . . an allegedly omnipotent but entirely isolated God could not have created the universe. Odd!

Fortunately, we can avoid these odd conclusions yet retain Hartshorne's commonsense claims that all creatures exert power and power is social. We can believe God created at the beginning of our universe and continues to create alongside creatures today. To do so, however, we must abandon omnipotence understood as God *ever* exerting all power. We must reject the idea that God creates in isolation, even at the start of our universe. In other words, God never exists without creation and never has a monopoly on power. I'll expand on these ideas later.

---

30. Bernard Loomer differentiates what he calls "linear" or "unilateral" power from "relational" power. The latter is what Hartshorne means by saying power is social. See Loomer, "Two Conceptions of Power," *Process Studies*, 6:1 (Spring 1976), 5-32.

31. Hartshorne, *The Divine Relativity*, 138. See also Simon Kittle, "God is (probably) a cause among causes," *Theology and Science* 22:2 (2022): 247-262.

32. Thomas Aquinas and Paul Tillich are among those who try to evade the problems of omnipotence by claiming God is not one power alongside others. Instead, they say, God is but "pure act" or "being itself." These are forms of apophatic theology, which tell us nothing constructive about God's activity in relation to creaturely activity. In a later section of this book, I argue that absolute apophatic theology is vacuous.

God Cannot Change Time

God's relation to time has long intrigued theologians. It surprises many who enter these conversations to learn that leading theologians of yesteryear and today say God can't change past events. What's done is done and cannot be altered, even by God.[33]

Thomas Aquinas, agreeing with both Aristotle and Augustine, says God cannot change the past. "That the past should not have been," Aquinas says, "does not come under the scope of divine power." He adds, "Some things at one time were in the nature of possibility, whilst they were yet to be done, which now fall short of the nature of possibility, when they have been done. So God is said not to be able to do them, because they themselves cannot be done."[34] John Wesley applies this to past divine actions: God "cannot . . . undo what he has done."[35]

Theologians offer various reasons why God cannot change the past. Some think God is timeless and has no past that could be changed. In this case, "past" is not a category for divine action.[36] Others say the past is real, but changing it requires doing what is ontologically impossible.[37] This argument says it's the nature of time to flow forward temporally, and it cannot

---

33. Jonathan Edwards puts it this way: "In explaining the nature of necessity, that in things which are past, their past existence is now necessary" (Jonathan Edwards, *Freedom of the Will*, s.12 [New York: Leavitt & Allen, 1857], 10.). On why most scholars say God cannot change the past, see Ronald H. Nash, *The Concept of God* (Grand Rapids, Mich.: Eerdmans, 1983); Alvin Plantinga, "On Ockham's Way Out," *Faith and Philosophy*, 3.3 (July 1986): 235-269; Roger Olson, "Can God Change the Past?" https://www.patheos.com/blogs/rogereolson/2021/06/can-god-change-the-past-2/ (Accessed 12/6/21)

34. Thomas Aquinas, *Summa Theologica*, 1a, Q. 25, A. 4.

35. Wesley, "On Divine Providence," Sermon 67, §§ 15, *Works*, 2: 541.

36. Edward Wierenga affirms divine timelessness but argues that God's goodness prevents God from changing the past. See Wierenga, *The Nature of God: An Inquiry into Divine Attributes* (Ithaca: Cornell University Press, 1989). Paul Helm argues that what is past for us is not so for God in *Eternal God* (Oxford: Oxford University Press, 1988).

37. For an example, see Thomas Flint and A. J. Freddoso, "Maximal Power," in *The Existence and Nature of God*, A. J. Freddoso, ed. (Notre Dame University Press, 1983).

be stopped or reversed. Existence is essentially time-indexed. Although these two views differ significantly, they do share this conclusion:

God cannot change the past.

Fewer theologians have written about God changing the future, but the same principles apply. Those who think a timeless God has no divine future should claim God cannot change it.[38] Those who say God moves with the forward flow of time should say there is no future to change. Only the present exists. For this latter group, God and creation engage a real but a not yet actual realm of possibilities.[39] In either case, however, theologians should further qualify omnipotence:

---

38. For a powerful argument against divine timelessness, see R. T. Mullins, *The End of the Timeless God* (Oxford: Oxford University Press, 2016). I'm also grateful to Mullins for his sharing from his manuscript in process, *From Divine Timemaker to Divine Watchmaker*. William Hasker argues that simple foreknowledge provides no providential advantage in "Why Simple Foreknowledge is Still Useless," *Journal of the Evangelical Theological Society* 52:3 (2007).

39. For philosophically-oriented works on God and time in open and relational thought, see David Basinger, *The Case for Freewill Theism: A Philosophical Assessment* (Downers Grove, Ill.: 1996); Daniel A. Dombrowski, *Analytic Theism, Hartshorne, and the Concept of God* (Albany, NY: State University of New York Press, 1996); selections from Gregory E. Ganssle and David M. Woodruff, eds, *God and Time: Essays on the Divine Nature* (New York: Oxford University Press, 2002); William Hasker, *God, Time, and Knowledge* (Ithaca, NY: Cornell University Press, 1989); Timothy O'Connor, *Theism and Ultimate Explanation: The Necessary Shape of Contingency* (London: Wiley-Blackwell, 2012); Alan Rhoda, "Beyond the Chessmaster Analogy: Game Theory and Divine Providence," in *Creation Made Free: Open Theology Engaging Science*, Thomas Jay Oord, ed., (Eugene, Or: Pickwick, 2009); George W. Shields and Donald W. Viney, "The Logic of Future Contingents" in *Process and Analysis: Whitehead, Hartshorne, and the Analytic Tradition*, George W. Shields, ed., (Albany, NY: State University of New York Press, 2004), 209–246; Richard Swinburne, *The Coherence of Theism* (Oxford: Oxford University Press, 1977); Dale Tuggy, "Three Roads to Open Theism," *Faith and Philosophy*, 24: (2007): 28–51; Donald Wayne Viney, "God Only Knows? Hartshorne and the Mechanics of Omniscience" in *Hartshorne, Process Philosophy and Theology*, Robert Kane and Stephen Phillips, eds. (Albany, NY: State University of New York Press, 1989), 71–90; Keith Ward, *God, Chance, and Necessity* (Oxford: Oneworld, 1996); *By Faith and Reason: The Essential Keith Ward*, Wm. Curtis Holtzen and Roberto Sirvent, eds. (London: Darton, Longman, and Todd, 2012); Nicholas Wolterstorff, "God Everlasting" in *Philosophy and Faith*, David Shatz, ed. (New York: McGraw, 2002), 62-69.

God cannot change the future.

For obvious reasons, ancient theologians did not address the scientific discoveries of recent centuries. Two especially important discoveries have been the slow evolutionary emergence of complex life forms from less complex ones and the very old age of the universe.[40] Augustine couldn't know, for instance, that the universe began roughly 13.8 billion years ago. Nor could he know about the vast amounts of time required for complex species to evolve from basic life forms.

The reality of evolution and the ancient age of the universe are not death knells for omnipotence. A theist might think God exerted all power when creating our universe long ago. Or that God creates through omnipotent control during a long evolutionary process. These claims run into the problems related to divine control I cited earlier, of course, but one might affirm them alongside other meanings of omnipotence.[41]

The vast time it took for the universe to arrive at its present state and the lengthy struggle required for life to become complex, however, should prompt us to ask questions about the overall credibility of omnipotence. If theologians are correct that God wanted companions capable of love, why would God wait billions of years to create complex lovers? If God's primary goal was the existence of people capable of giving the Godhead glory, why not instantaneously create worship-capable humans?

The amount and extent of creaturely suffering in evolutionary history also raises questions about omnipotence. If God could have created the world we live in without subjecting countless creatures to suffering in

---

40. A number of excellent books on God and evolution have been written. See, for instance, Ilia Delio, *Christ in Evolution* (New Jersey: Orbis, 2011); John Haught, *God After Darwin* (Routledge, 2007); Matthew Hill, *Evolution and Holiness* (Downers Grove, Ill.: IVP Academic, 2016).

41. Riichiro Hoashi addresses these issues in *The Problem of Omnipotence in Current Theology* (University of Chicago, 1918).

evolutionary history, why wouldn't a loving God skip the lengthy process of pain? Doesn't God care about animals and their suffering?[42]

The age of the universe intensifies a longstanding set of questions. Assuming God created the universe from nothing about 13.8 billion years ago, why didn't God create *sooner*? An omnipotent God could apparently create whenever. Why not earlier? Or later?

And what motivated God to create in the first place? Did this motivation emerge in God, which meant God changed? Or was it there all along? And if it was, we return to the question of creating sooner. Choosing one of these answers also raises additional questions about divine immutability that most theologies affirming omnipotence are ill-equipped to handle.

The most common response to hard questions like these is to appeal to what is "fitting" for God. Few theologians address what "fitting" means, of course. "God has His reasons," they say. In other words, the mystery card.

A growing number of theologians think the vast age of the universe and the reality of evolution align better with the view God that always creates alongside creaturely others. And with the view that God cannot create complex creatures instantly. In other words, discoveries in science are changing how we might think about God as Creator.[43] But in order for these views to make good sense, theologians must reject God as omnipotent.

However one answers the difficult questions of creation, the evidence of an old universe and an evolutionary process on earth at least point to qualifications that time itself places on God. We might put those qualifications this way:

---

42. Some of the more influential attempts to answer this question come from Richard Swinburne and John Hick. See Swinburne, *Providence and the Problem of Evil* (Oxford: Clarendon, 1998); Hick, *Evil and the God of Love*, rev. ed. (New York: Harper and Row, 1978).

43. Most of the leading voices in this theological exploration come from the process theology tradition. As an example, see David Ray Griffin, "Creation out of Nothing, Creation out of Chaos, and the Problem of Evil," *Encountering Evil*, Stephen T. Davis, ed. 2nd ed. (Louisville: Westminster John Knox, 2001).

God cannot create a universe billions of years old and the same universe not billions of years old.

God cannot create a complex creature through an evolutionary process and that same complex creature instantly.

These denials are similar to a claim by St. Jerome. He said God "cannot bring it about that a woman who was seduced was not seduced."[44] Thomas Aquinas agreed and said, "the fact that she had been seduced cannot be removed from her."[45] This seduction example pertains to a creature's relation to time. Applied to the old universe and evolution, this means God can't create the actual universe as both old and not old. And the evolutionary process through which God creates cannot be both slow and instantaneous.

Time qualifies omnipotence.

God Cannot Control Free Creatures and Chance Events

Philosophers and theologians have long wrestled with the relationship between God's power and human freedom.[46] The compatibilist claim that God exerts all power, but free creatures exert some is, as we saw in the previous chapter, incoherent. But this does not mean creaturely freedom is boundless. Authentic free will—what philosophers typically call

---

44. The misogynistic tone of this claim will strike many modern ears as offensive. But we can change this to a man being seduced and retain the meaning important to my argument.

45. Thomas Aquinas, *Summa Theologica*, I, q. 25, a. 4. See also the discussion of this by Joshua Hoffman and Gary Rosenkrantz, "Omnipotence," in *A Companion to Philosophy of Religion*, Philip L. Quinn and Charles Taliaferro, eds. (Malden, Mass.: Blackwell, 1999), 231.

46. In the contemporary era, Alvin Plantinga's work on libertarian free will has been especially influential. See his *God, Freedom, and Evil* (Grand Rapids, Mich.: Eerdmans, 1974). See also Thomas Flint & A. J. Freddoso, "Maximal Power," in *The Existence and Nature of God*.

"libertarian freedom"—is limited by a host of actors, factors, forces, and possibilities.

If creaturely freedom involves creatures exerting power, God cannot be omnipotent in the sense of exerting *all* power.[47] If such freedom involves creatures exerting self-causation, God cannot be omnipotent in the sense of being the sufficient cause of what free creatures do.

Leigh Vicens and Simon Kittle explain the issue succinctly: "It must *not* be possible for God to determine what a created person freely chooses."[48] C. S. Lewis puts the point this way: "If you choose to say 'God can give a creature free will and at the same time withhold free will from it,' you have not succeeded in saying *anything* about God: meaningless combinations of words do not suddenly acquire meaning simply because we prefix to them the two other words 'God can.'"[49] I addressed these qualifications in the previous scripture chapter, but let me note them here:

God cannot exert all power and creatures exert some power.

God cannot be the only cause and creatures have self-causation.

Many theists believe God is *essentially* omnipotent but voluntarily chooses to self-limit. Although God could have made creatures without the power necessary for free choices, God did not want a universe of completely determined robots. God wanted real give-and-receive relationships. So . . . God voluntarily qualifies divine power.

---

47. On the ultimacy of freedom, see Jeffery F. Keuss, *Freedom of the Self: Kenosis, Cultural Identity, and Mission at the Crossroads* (Eugene, Or.: Pickwick, 2010); Christian J. Barrigar, *Freedom All the Way Up* (Victoria, B.C.: Friesen, 2017).

48. Leigh C. Vicens and Simon Kittle, *God and Human Freedom* (Cambridge University Press, 2019), 40.

49. C.S. Lewis, *The Problem of Pain* (San Francisco: HarperSanFrancisco, 2001), 18.

The notion that God voluntarily self-limits falters in the face of suffering and evil, as we'll see in the next chapter. But it's important to note here an often overlooked qualification to omnipotence implied in the "God is voluntarily self-limiting" view. God can't be both omnipotent and control real relationships with free moral creatures.[50] If God thinks relationships with free moral agents desirable, God cannot exert all power. Alvin Plantinga puts it in the positive sense: "God can create a world containing moral good only by creating significantly free persons."[51] We might put it this way:

God cannot both control creatures and relate with free moral creatures.

One of the results of God giving freedom, say many theologians, is that creatures sometimes misuse that freedom. They sin. Apparently, God cannot create free creatures without also creating them with the ability to use freedom wrongly. John Hick explains: God "cannot without contradiction be conceived to have so constituted men that they could be guaranteed freely to respond to Himself in authentic faith and love and worship."[52]

If God could have created free creatures without the possibility of their sinning, one would think a loving God would do so. But apparently creaturely freedom requires the possibility of doing good or evil. Another way to say this is that God did not create humans who are, by necessity, morally perfect.[53] We might express these qualifications like this:

---

50. On this, see Patrick Todd, "Does God Have the Moral Standing to Blame?" *Faith and Philosophy, 35:1* (2018), 33–55.

51. Plantinga, *God, Freedom, and Evil*, 235.

52. See Hick, *Evil and the God of Love*, 275.

53. This argument comes in many forms. Perhaps the most influential version is offered by Plantinga in *God, Freedom, and Evil*.

God cannot create free creatures unable to sin.

God cannot create morally perfect beings who are also free.

Those who take creaturely freedom as something God cannot control often regard chance events as beyond divine control. Of course, if events that we think are random are really entirely determined by God, then they are not chance or random. They're divinely determined. But if some events—among creatures, genes, or quantum level—are genuinely chance or random, they must not be controlled by anyone. They are, therefore, *not* events an omnipotent God controls.

J. L. Mackie puts the issue like this: "Can an omnipotent being make things which he cannot control? . . . If the answer is 'Yes' it follows that if God actually makes things which he cannot control, he is not omnipotent once he has made them: there are then things which he cannot do."[54] I'll put it this way:

God cannot control chance or random events.

Qualifying omnipotence by saying God can't control free creatures and chance events is significant and the implications profound. Some theists continue to call God omnipotent despite admitting these inabilities. Others say the qualifications undermine the meaning of omnipotence altogether. After all, it seems odd to say, "God is omnipotent but can't control free creatures or stop random events."

54. J. L. Mackie, "Evil and Omnipotence," *Mind* 64 (1955), 210.

An Incorporeal God Cannot Lift a Pebble

Another qualification to omnipotence technically fits among activities God can't do given the divine nature. Qualifications in my earlier discussion included limitations such as God cannot lie, cannot stop existing, cannot be absent, cannot stop loving, and more.

The qualification I have in mind here pertains to what theologians call God's "incorporeality." Most have thought God is essentially a universal spirit without a localized divine body. God is bodiless. Theologians and writers of scripture compare God's "composition" to wind, gravity, ether, souls, or minds. Many say God has no materiality. The result of these traditional claims, however, is that God does not have a divine body. And a bodiless God cannot activities that embodied creatures can. As Charles Taliaferro puts it, "If God is nonphysical, then . . . God cannot do certain actions that require a body."[55]

For instance, the universal divine Spirit does not have a divine hand to throw snowballs, smash sandcastles, or hold cups of coffee. God can't curl a dumbbell, tackle a quarterback, throw a dirt clod, or kick a soccer ball. God can't plant a seed with a divine hand, raise a spoon of ice cream, or do pushups. To return to this chapter's initial qualification, an incorporeal God can't lift *a pebble*, let alone a big rock!

The limits to an incorporeal God extend beyond having no literal hands. God also has no legs, no mouth, no wings, no fins, no teeth, and so on. Consequently, we can imagine thousands upon thousands of qualifications for an incorporeal Spirit without a localized divine body. And thousands upon thousands of activities creatures can do but God cannot. Here are just a few:

---

55. Taliaferro, *A Contemporary Philosophy of Religion*, 71.

God cannot lift a pebble.

God cannot bench press 50 pounds.

God cannot sit on a nest.

God cannot chew licorice.

God cannot do pushups.

"But God can do those things *through creatures*," someone might respond. God acts through us and creation. We're God's hands and feet.

This response makes no sense, however, if one thinks God cannot control free creatures and other agents. See the earlier discussion. If creatures have real freedom and agency to use their bodies as they like (assuming natural limits), God can't control them. Those creaturely bodies aren't literally divine, so creatures don't literally become God's hands and feet.

Creatures can freely collaborate with God, however. When responding to the divine call, they can use their bodies, wings, fins, feet, teeth, and more to cooperate as God's *metaphorical* bodies. But these activities are not done by God's literal body. Creatures with freedom and agency can also resist God's inspiration and fail to cooperate.

Saying an incorporeal God does these activities and thousands more *through* creaturely bodies only makes sense if 1) we are not claiming creatures are divine and 2) creatures freely cooperate with God. But this isn't an exercise of God's omnipotence.

In sum, a bodiless God cannot do thousands and thousands of activities that embodied creatures can. These qualifications to omnipotence are far-reaching, and I'll return to them when addressing the problem of evil.[56]

---

56. Some will wonder if the incarnation of God in Jesus Christ is an exception to what I've written here. It is not an exception if one believes Jesus had the freedom to cooperate (or not) with God. For a spirit-Christology that says Jesus freely cooperated with the divine Spirit, see Thomas Jay Oord, "Essential Kenosis Christology," in *Methodist Christology*.

God Can Do Whatever God Wants?

Most intellectually sophisticated theologians acknowledge the qualifications I list in this chapter. At least most of them.[57] But some will still say, "An omnipotent God can do whatever He wants to do." Augustine puts it this way: "God does whatsoever He will: that is omnipotence."[58]

Two passages in the Psalms have been translated in ways that support the idea that God does whatever God wants: "Our God is in the heavens; he does whatever he pleases" (115:3; 135:6). Charles Hodge puts it more clearly: "God can do whatever He wills. . . . This simple idea of the omnipotence of God, that He can do without effort, and by a volition whatever He wills, is the highest conceivable idea of power."[59]

At first, this may sound identical to the "God can do anything" view that requires thousands of qualifications. But it's slightly different. It says God can do whatever God *wants* to do. Hodge highlights the distinction when he mentions God's "volition." There's a difference between "God can do all things" and "God can do whatever He *wants*." The latter emphasizes divine choice and desire.

"God can do whatever He wants" sounds impressive. But it isn't. Upon examination, we'll find it barren. It adds little to questions about God's abilities and activities, if anything. It's as illuminating as saying, "God can do all things compatible with God's nature," which isn't illuminating once scrutinized. It's like saying, "Alexa can do whatever Alexa can do."

Let me explain by asking a question: Would a perfectly wise God decide to stop existing?

Hodge and others would answer that a perfectly wise God would never *want* to stop existing. God knows that God exists necessarily, and

---

57. Vicens and Kittle address many of these issues and offer a short list of qualifications in *God and Human Freedom.*

58. Augustine, *Sermo de symbolo ad catechumenos* 2 (CChr.SL 46, 185-6, PL), 40.

59. Hodge, *Systematic Theology,* Vol I, 407.

nothing can end God's existence, even God. Therefore, a perfectly wise God would not desire to do what, in principle, cannot be done. Doing so goes against God's nature.

We can add to this the entire roster of qualifications I've listed thus far. A perfectly wise God would never *want* to make 2 + 2 = 7, for instance, because God knows it's impossible. An omniscient God who necessarily knows everything knowable would not *want* to be ignorant. An omnipresent God necessarily present to all creation would not *want* to be absent from Chicago. A perfectly wise God would not *want* to control free will creatures, because this God knows controlling free beings is impossible. God wouldn't *want* to control chance events that cannot, in principle, be controlled. A perfectly wise God would not *want* to lift a rock with a divine hand or swim the ocean as a fish-God. And so on.

"God can do whatever God wants" is empty puff. It tickles the ears of those who like saying, "God is omnipotently sovereign" or "God is in control." But all the qualifications I listed and thousands more render it hollow.

A perfectly wise God would not want to do what God cannot do.

God Cannot Be Meaninglessly Omnipotent

In order to avoid qualifying omnipotence, some claim God's power is *entirely* unlike anything we know. I call this "absolute apophatic theology." It claims that nothing we say, think, write, feel, or experience tells us truth about God.[60] An apophatic theologian may affirm omnipotence but say the word is not true of God in any sense we could understand, because

---

60. I'm differentiating "absolute apophatic theology" from mere apophatic theology. Many consider the latter to mean we cannot be certain about what we say of God or know God fully. Those who embrace mere apophatic theology may say we can know *something* about God, however, or that our words about God may express a *measure* of truth. I affirm that version of apophatic theology. Absolute apophatic theology denies *all* positive knowledge of God.

God is beyond understanding. God is all-powerful, according to this view, but mysteriously so.

I don't take absolute apophatic theology seriously, because it's meaningless. Those who make such claims are misguided. After all, if "God is omnipotent" has no meaning we can recognize, we have no justification to say, "God is omnipotent." Absolute apophatic theologians should remain silent. Yet many speak, even though it's self-refuting to say, "Words about God cannot be true" alongside "God is omnipotent." I'll put it this way:

God cannot be meaninglessly omnipotent.

A more reasonable claim is that omnipotence is meaningful only when qualified in the ways I've been noting. This has been standard practice among theologians and theistic philosophers in the past and present, although I know of no list of qualifications to omnipotence exactly like what I've given here. The sheer number of modifications, restrictions, provisos, and limits required for omnipotence to be meaningful, however, is staggering! The sheer number, I believe, undercuts any good reason to say, "God is omnipotent."

Let me offer an analogy. Suppose I said a place in Idaho is "all-glorious." I might even say it's "omni-glorious," to coin a word. But suppose upon claiming the site is all-glorious, I identify dozens, hundreds, or thousands of ways it is *not* glorious. My list includes exceptions, qualifications, and limits. Those listening to me would rightly doubt the accuracy of the label "all-glorious." The place cannot be *all* glorious if there are thousands of ways it is not.

Analogously, identifying the thousands of activities an omnipotent God *cannot* do should compel us to reject the claim "God is omnipotent." It's not warranted. The same goes for calling God "all-powerful," "sovereign," or "almighty," if those words are understood as synonyms for omnipotence.[61] God simply *can't* do countless actions, including thousands that you and I can.

Omnipotence connotes to many people the ability to do anything, an ability that is, at least on its face, inherently unqualified. Consequently, the practice of qualifying omnipotence—which just about every serious theologian and theistic philosopher does—makes little sense. Qualifying a word that, by definition, means "without qualification" confuses and misleads.

Qualified omnipotence is an oxymoron.

Conclusion

In this chapter, I've listed many things God cannot do and called them qualifications to omnipotence. Here they are again . . .

God cannot make a mountain so high God cannot climb it.

God cannot make a creature so small God cannot find it.

God cannot make a river so wide God cannot cross it.

God cannot create a jail so secure God cannot escape it.

God cannot make 2 + 2 = 1.

God cannot make 24 ÷ 12 = 47791.

God cannot make 3 x 4 = 110,093.

God cannot add two integers and get a fraction.

God cannot make a round square.

---

61. Peter Geach argues for a difference between almightiness and omnipotence. See "Omnipotence," *Philosophy* 43 (1973), 7-20. I've offered meanings of "almighty" that differ from omnipotence. See Oord, *Pluriform Love*, ch 7. Most theists, however, use "omnipotent" and "almighty" interchangeably.

God cannot create a triangle whose angles do not add up to 180°.

God cannot make the circumference of a circle 5nr.

God cannot make the area of a rectangle base x height x 67.

God cannot make something both "A" and "Not A."

God cannot make a married bachelor.

God cannot make a hornless unicorn.

God cannot make a living cadaver.

God cannot die.

God cannot sin.

God cannot lie.

God cannot be deceived.

God cannot decide to stop existing.

God cannot be omnipresent and absent somewhere.

God cannot be omniscient and ignorant of some fact.

God cannot be all-loving but fail to love someone.

God cannot create someone smarter than God.

God cannot create someone stronger than God.

God cannot create someone more loving than God.

God cannot create an infinite divine being.

God cannot decide to change, because God is immutable.

God cannot be affected by creatures, because God is impassible.

God cannot experience the flow of time, because God is timeless.

God cannot feel emotion in response to creatures, because God has no such emotions.

God cannot create God's nature.

God cannot change the past.

God cannot change the future.

God cannot create a universe billions of years old and the same universe not billions of years old.

God cannot create a complex creature through an evolutionary process and create that same complex creature instantly.

God cannot exert all power and creatures exert some power.

God cannot be the only cause and creatures have self-causation.

God cannot both control creatures and relate with free moral creatures.

God cannot create free creatures unable to sin.

God cannot create morally perfect beings who are also free.

God cannot control chance or random events.

God cannot lift a pebble.

God cannot bench press 50 pounds.

God cannot sit on a nest.

God cannot chew licorice.

God cannot do pushups.

God cannot be meaninglessly omnipotent.

A comprehensive list would include thousands, millions, and perhaps billions of qualifications. Examples on that list fall under numerous broad categories. For instance, God cannot do what is illogical or ontologically contradictory. God can't act in ways that oppose math and geometry. God cannot do many things humans can, because those activities oppose God's nature. God cannot make duplicates of God or other beings with superior abilities. God's relation to time and creation entails limits on what God can do. These limits expand if we believe God creates genuinely free creatures. They expand more if we take seriously claims about God's real relations with creation and chance events in the universe. They expand yet more if God is incorporeal and cannot do activities creatures with bodies can. And more.

I began this chapter with an experience from my university philosophy class. I close with an experience in a religion class. I and my fellow students read a little book by J. B. Phillips called, *Your God is Too Small*. Although the book cleverly describes bad views of God, Phillips fails to realize that many people imagine a God that's too big! In their attempts to describe God's immense power, believers unwisely embrace omnipotence. The most thoughtful eventually realize the word requires numerous disclaimers, stipulations, exceptions, and provisos. An omnipotent God is too big to be intelligible.

Impressive work has been done by specialists to qualify and nuance omnipotence, attempting to make it credible. But attempts to salvage omnipotence do not match what 99.99% of people—both scholars and laity—mean by "God is omnipotent."[62] I agree with Wes Morriston that

---

62. Some philosophers try to account for these qualifications by formulating complicated theorems. Thomas Flint and A. J. Freddoso offer an example: "S is omnipotent at t in W if and only if for any state of affairs p and world-type-for-S Ls such that p is not a member of Ls, if there is a world W∗ such that Ls is true in both W and W∗, and W∗ shares the same history with W at t, and at t in W∗ someone actualizes p, then S has the power at t in W to actualize p." Flint & Freddoso, "Maximal Power," 99. This attempt and others like it are unconvincing. They fail to account for some of the necessary categories of qualification. And they don't fit what most people—professional theologians and everyday believers—mean when they claim God is omnipotent.

specialized efforts "employ so much technical apparatus and contain so many subordinate clauses and qualifications that it is natural to wonder whether they have much to do with what an ordinary person might mean by saying that God is all-powerful."[63]

Based on the *enormous* number of necessary qualifications, I believe theists should stop saying, "God is omnipotent." The phrase should be dead to them. Believers should also not say, "God is all-powerful." Add to the problem of copious qualifications that omnipotence signals to many people the lack of any limitation, and this chapter's title is further justified: omnipotence dies a death by a thousand qualifications.

It's time to commit dictiocide: to kill "omnipotence."

Rather than embrace omnipotence, it makes more sense to consider the kind of power a loving God might have.[64] God can still be thought to express immense power and be the greatest conceivable being. Divine power can still be considered perfect or maximal.[65] But these legitimate ways to understand God's power do not require belief in omnipotence.[66]

Later in this book, I propose an alternative view of divine power. My alternative denies omnipotence and considers love logically first among divine attributes. It does *not* say God controls, exerts all power, or can do

---

63. Wes Morriston, "Omnipotence and the Power to Choose: A Reply to Wielenberg," *Faith and Philosophy*, 19:3 (July 2002), 358.

64. The comparative approach has the most promise when it comes to talking about divine power.

65. I align with Yujin Nagasawa's "maximal God thesis," whereby God has a maximal and consistent set of attributes pertaining to knowledge, power, love, and more. I'm convinced that classical views of omnipotence, omniscience, and even omnibenevolence, as typically understood, should be jettisoned. As I argue in the final chapter, I think love is the logically primary divine attribute. See Nagasawa, *Maximal God* (Oxford: Oxford University Press, 2017).

66. On perfect and maximal power, see Flint and Freddoso, "Maximal Power," in *The Existence and Nature of God*; Joshua Hoffman and Gary Rosenkrantz, "Omnipotence," in *A Companion to Philosophy of Religion*, 229-235; Wierenga, *The Nature of God*.

absolutely anything. But it *does* say God is powerful. Even if some readers do not accept my alternative, what I've argued here and in the previous chapter should persuade them to join me at the graveside of omnipotence.

We should change the children's song to *Our God is so big, so strong, and so mighty but **there are many things** God cannot do!*

3

Evil Ends Omnipotence

I now turn to what we all know first-hand: hurt and harm. Experiences of pointless pain and unnecessary suffering lead some to doubt God is in control. Evil leads others to doubt God exists at all. In either case, evil ends omnipotence.

The problem of evil comes in many forms, but it rests on three basic claims: 1) genuine evil occurs; 2) God loves all creation; 3) God is omnipotent. Just about everyone affirms God as loving, although what "loving" means varies depending on the theologian. In many theologies, divine love is nonrelational, vengeful, completely self-centered, unemotional, and entirely unlike our love, which makes the phrase "God loves all creation" unintelligible.[1] But even these disjointed theologies struggle to make sense of evil.

In subtle or obvious ways, many believers deny the first claim in the problem of evil. They think hurt and harm are part of a divine plan, and God allows pain for some greater good. If true, there is no *genuine* evil, in

---

1. I explain in an academic way the problems with classical views of God's love and offer more plausible views in *Pluriform Love*. I offer a more accessible explanation in *Open and Relational Theology*, ch. 6.

the sense of events that make the world, all things considered, worse than it might have been.[2]

Eventually, most believers play the mystery card when faced with evil. They affirm each basic claim in the problem but admit they cannot understand how all three are true together. As a result, confusion reigns.

In this chapter, I explain why the problem of evil buries omnipotence. Believing God is both loving and omnipotent is incompatible with the evidence of evil. Rather than chalk up this crucial issue to mystery or reject belief in God altogether, I offer a *solution*. This solution has six dimensions, each rejecting omnipotence. Scrapping the idea that God is all-powerful clears a path for overcoming the primary reason why atheists say they don't believe in God and the primary confusion for believers who do.[3] And it solves other problems that stymy inquiring minds.

Omnipotence is not born of scripture, and it dies a death of a thousand qualifications in philosophy. Evil buries the corpse six feet under. But the death of omnipotence is not the death of God.[4]

Why Doesn't God Prevent Evil?

Gallup polls of the 1940s, 50s, and 60s indicate that 98% of Americans believed in God during these decades. Cultural references to divinity supported those surveys, and in most public places, belief was assumed. The

---

2. David Ray Griffin defines genuine evil this way in *God, Power, and Evil: A Process Theodicy* (Louisville, KY: Westminster John Knox, 2004). I contrast genuine evil with so-called "necessary evil" in *The Uncontrolling Love of God*, ch. 3.

3. Find popular explanations of my solution to the problem of evil in *God Can't: How to Believe in God and Love after Tragedy, Abuse, and Suffering* (Grasmere, Id.: SacraSage, 2019) and *Questions and Answers for God Can't*. My corresponding academic books are *The Uncontrolling Love of God* and *Pluriform Love*.

4. A significant body of literature explores "the death of God," a label made famous by Thomas J.J. Altizer and others. Some of those writings advocate reductive atheism. Other death of God writers simply oppose theologies that make no sense of reality or are internally inconsistent. For an edited collection of essays exploring this, see Daniel J. Peterson and Michael Zbaraschuk, eds. *Resurrecting the Death of God* (Albany, NY: SUNY, 2015).

percentages of European believers was slipping during that time but remained relatively high compared to today. At least in the Western world, belief in God was common.

A Gallup poll taken in the 2020s indicated that the percentage of American believers dropped to 81%.[5] Young and educated Americans were least likely to think God exists, but belief decreased in nearly every category. If this poll correctly reflects America, sixty million Americans considered themselves nonbelievers of one type or another. Polls show the overall number and percentage of nonbelievers in Europe as even higher, despite a rich history of theological reflection.[6]

Little research has been done on *why* people do not believe in God.[7] But in conversation after conversation—with both intellectuals and everyday people—the problem of evil stands out. "If an omnipotent and loving God exists," people wonder, "why doesn't this almighty One prevent pointless pain, unnecessary suffering, and untold horrors?"

Because evil exists, millions conclude God does not.

Believers respond to the challenge with various answers. Some claim God causes or allows evil to punish sin.[8] Others say God wanted a world of hardship as a training ground for character development.[9] Some blame evil on Satan and demons but say God is allowing their dastardly deeds, at least

---

5. Jeffrey M. Jones, "Belief in God in U.S. Dips to 81%, a New Low" https://news.gallup.com/poll/393737/belief-god-dips-new-low.aspx (Accessed 12/29/22)

6. For Pew research on atheism in general and Europe in particular, see Michael Lipka, "10 facts about atheists." https://www.pewresearch.org/fact-tank/2019/12/06/10-facts-about-atheists/ (Accessed 12/29/22).

7. I make this claim after searching for credible polls and sources. If readers know of reputable studies on reasons unbelievers give for rejecting God, I would appreciate being informed of them.

8. Bart D. Ehrman explores this "answer" to evil as it arises in the Bible. Ehrman argues convincingly that it is not a solution. See *God's Problem: How the Bible Fails to Answer Our Most Important Question—Why We Suffer* (New York: HarperCollins, 2008).

9. John Hick offers the most influential contemporary form of this argument in *Evil and the God of Love.* One of the best criticisms of this view comes from C. Robert Mesle, *John Hick's Theodicy: A Process Humanist Critique* (London: MacMillan, 1991).

for a time.[10] Some claim God allows evil in order to reach a world-building goal or secure some greater good. Others say God wants creatures to be free, which outweighs God's desire to help victims of rape, murder, and abuse. And so on.

The answers typically given to the problem of evil fail to convince most people . . . including most believers. Many answers portray God as less than consistently loving, or they imply suffering is less than genuinely evil. Some "answers" are bald appeals to inscrutability. Many believers would rather play the mystery card than rethink their view of God.

In scholarly circles, some who appeal to mystery adopt the label "skeptical theists." They acknowledge the reality of evil and affirm the existence of a good and omnipotent God. But they're skeptical the problem of evil can be solved. On an issue that compels hundreds of millions to reject God, skeptical theists offer nothing constructive.[11]

A God who can control others, who can do absolutely anything, or who has all power can prevent evil singlehandedly. This omnipotent One requires no help from others, and its will cannot be thwarted. An all-powerful deity who created the universe from nothing also created the fundamental laws and conditions that cause evil. This Creator can interrupt, interfere, or intervene in the natural world.

Catherine Keller identifies the omnipotence logic leading many to unbelief: "*If* God could have prevented but 'let' this horror happen, this child's painful death, this ancestor's enslavement, this people's holocaust, for His own inscrutable reasons—to teach, to punish, to test," she says,

---

10. John Piper is among those who support this view. See "Why Does God Allow Satan to Live?" https://www.desiringgod.org/interviews/why-does-god-allow-satan-to-live (Accessed 1/31/2023).

11. I find the skeptical theist appeal to mystery especially unsatisfying. For a concise presentation of the view, see Stephen Wykstra, "A Skeptical Theist View," in *God and the Problem of Evil: Five Views*, Chad Meister and James K. Dew, Jr., eds. (Downers Grove, Ill.: Intervarsity, 2017). See my response to Wykstra in the same book.

"*then* atheism is the only answer."[12] Daniel Migliore puts it this way: "The horrors of slavery, genocides, concentration camps, and other atrocities of modern warfare have made it not only intellectually difficult but also morally reprehensible to believe in the omnipotent God of much traditional theology."[13]

Some stop believing when they experience evils personally. Survivors of rape, torture, abuse, and other cruelty wonder why an omnipotent God failed to prevent their horrors. When evil is personal, doubt is greatest, because we can easily see better alternatives. "A loving and omnipotent God *could* and *should* have stopped what I endured!" we say. And we're right.

The evils of natural disasters and disease raise additional questions. Reflective people wonder why an omnipotent God doesn't intervene to prevent flooding, hurricanes, disease, genetic disorders, or pandemics. Doing so would not require overriding free will, at least not in most cases. "If God created all that exists," many wonder, "why doesn't He stop natural evils?" It's a good question.

Still other evils emerge from social and political systems. If omnipotent, God installs or permits all systems and leaders, including the unjust.[14] Belief in omnipotence at least indirectly supports tyranny and tyrants, which tears apart the relational fabric necessary for the common good. "An omnipotent God who *truly* loves would not allow political bullies to persecute us," some say. "Nor would a loving God uphold systems that crush us!" That's a reasonable conclusion.

A friend posted on social media what is true for many: "I have two words for why God is not omnipotent: 'Nazi Holocaust.'" Many in the 20th century asked questions about God's love and power in light of world

12. Catherine Keller, *Political Theology of the Earth* (Columbia University Press, 2018), 117.

13. Migliore, *The Power of God and the gods of Power*, 84.

14. The classic work in political theology showing the link between omnipotence and political systems is Carl Schmitt's book *Political Theology: Four Chapters on the Concept of Sovereignty,* George Schwab, trans. (Chicago: University of Chicago Press, 1985).

wars, brutal dictatorships, and genocides. Rabbi Irving Greenberg argues that to be adequate to life, theology must account for the holocaust's horrendous evils. "No statement, theological or otherwise," says Greenberg, "should be made that would not be credible in the presence of burning children."[15] Hans Jonas answers that challenge: "after Auschwitz, we can assert with greater force than ever that an omnipotent deity would have to be not good or . . . totally unintelligible."[16] Jonas rejects the problematic view of power: "This is not an omnipotent God."[17]

The breadth, depth, and frequency of evil lead many to stop believing an omnipotent God exists. Who can blame them?

Worshipping Omnipotence

Worship lyrics and liturgies both introduce and reinforce omnipotence. From an early age, many praise God as all-powerful; sermons, songs, and symbols say God is sovereign.[18] Day after day, week after week, believers corporately or individually praise God as able to do absolutely anything. For many, the words of worship are more influential than either scripture or philosophy when it comes to imagining divine power.

A common worship theme says God sits atop a hierarchy of power. God is the "King of kings," say many citing biblical language, and "Lord of

---

15. Irving Greenberg, "Cloud of Smoke, Pillar of Fire: Judaism, Christianity, and Modernity After the Holocaust," in Eva Fleischer, ed., Auschwitz: Beginning of a New Era? (New York: Ktav Publishing House, 1977), 23.

16. Hans Jonas, "The Concept of God after Auschwitz: A Jewish Voice," *The Journal of Religion* 67 (January 1987): 9-10.

17. Ibid., 8. See also, John C. Merkle, "Challenging the Idea of Divine Omnipotence: Jewish Voices and a Christian Response," *Journal of Ecumenical Studies*, 57:3 (Summer 2022), 422.

18. Copyright laws make it expensive for me to cite song lyrics that proclaim God as omnipotent. But I cited a few earlier. If they attend a few Christian worship services, readers should have little problem finding their own examples.

lords" (e.g., Ps. 136:2-3). In this view, it's easy to think a Divine Commander orchestrates a top-down chain of power, and all rulers and authorities in the chain carry out God's commands.[19]

Often accompanying claims about omnipotence are complementary claims about humans as passive subjects or obedient servants. When God is thought to exert *all* power, worshippers function as puppets, and God pulls the strings. When God is thought to control occasionally, worshippers must trust Omnipotence will guarantee what's *really* important. The implication, however, is that any evil we experience wasn't important enough for God to prevent.

It's even common for worshippers to say they've surrendered decision-making to the Almighty. "Take my will," some say, or "I'm only free when the Sovereign King controls me." The omnipotent God is large and in charge, and He rules over creatures whose power is either nonexistent or inconsequential.

Seeing God as omnipotent affects how believers think about political leaders and social policies. Carl Schmitt, the progenitor of political theology, argues that humans build political systems from assumptions about divine sovereignty. "All significant concepts of the modern theory of the state are secularized theological concepts," says Schmitt, "not only because of their historical development—in which they were transferred from theology to the theory of the state, whereby, for example, the omnipotent god became the omnipotent lawgiver—but also because of their systematic

---

19. Often, these commanders are male. This prompts Dorothee Soelle to wonder, "As a woman I have to ask why it is that human beings honor a God who most important attribute is power, whose prime need is to subjugate, whose greatest fear is equality?" And "why should we honor and love this being . . . if this being is in fact no more than an outsized man?" For her feminist critique, see *The Strength of the Weak: Toward a Christian Feminist Identity* (Philadelphia, PA: Fortress, 1984), 97. See also Nancy R. Howell, *A Feminist Cosmology* (Humanities Press, 2000) and Karen Winslow, *Imagining Equity* (Wesley's Foundery, 2021).

structure."[20] Doctrines of divine power shape views of creaturely power, both political heads and systems.

It's to be expected, of course, that our views of earthly rulers will also influence our views of the divine Leader. In fact, such influence is necessary if language about God as leader is to make sense. Without analogies between Creator and creatures, we can't talk plausibly about God. The question is, *Which* analogies make better sense of God as leader?

When worship rites and rituals describe God as King of kings, we are tempted to imagine God in the image of imperial rulers. That's what many in early Christianity did. As Alfred North Whitehead quips, "The church gave unto God the properties that belonged exclusively to Caesar."[21] Those properties often included absolute sovereignty. The practice of comparing a Divine Ruler to human rulers is, as Charles Hartshorne puts it, "perhaps the most shockingly bad of all theological analogies, or at least the one open to the most abuses."[22]

Similarly, when God is worshipped as King of kings and Lord of lords, it's natural to think political leaders should be afforded at least some of the privileges we afford God.[23] When we ask, "Who has unlimited power?"

---

20. Carl Schmitt, *Political Theology*, 36. See Catherine Keller's brilliant use of and response to Schmitt in *Political Theology of the Earth*.

21. Whitehead, *Process and Reality: An Essay in Cosmology*, Corrected edition by David Ray Griffin and Donald W. Sherburne (New York: Free, 1978 [1929]), 234. For an overview of Whitehead's view of religion, see Daniel A. Dombrowski, *Whitehead's Religious Thought* (Albany, NY: SUNY, 2017).

22. Hartshorne, *Omnipotence and Other Theological Mistakes*, 11.

23. Anna Case-Winters offers a feminist critique, arguing that God has traditionally been compared with dominant males. "The power implied here has been interpreted as power *in the mode of domination and control.*" Power as "over power" rather than "with power" is legitimized for humans, says Case-Winters, "with obvious disastrous results in the form of oppression, exploitation, and violence." In fact, "the prevailing model [of God's power] is shaped by a male bias, and the resulting way of meaning and living out power has had negative ramifications in the realm of human affairs." See *God's Power*, 19. One of the best overall introductions to and analysis of feminism is Monica A. Coleman, Nancy R. Howell, and Helene Talon Russell, eds., *Creating Women's Theology* (Eugene, Or.: Pickwick, 2011).

says Schmitt, we identify a king, president, prince, or some other power broker whom we regard as above the law. God and king are granted exceptions. In fact, the typical understanding of miracles assumes an omnipotent God occasionally breaks the laws of nature and controls humans. That's exceptional. Analogously, earthly sovereigns should be allowed to break social and moral laws that apply to the rest of us.[24]

History shows that most leaders crave power. When they get it, they wield power in coercive ways. History also shows that some citizens are attracted to power-hungry politicians, at least in the short term. They hope a strongman can, by fiat, solve their problems.[25]

Given these realities, it should not surprise us when worshippers project onto God their emperor's desire for authoritarian control. Nor should we be shocked when serfs or citizens want a god-like potentate to end their troubles singlehandedly.[26] Absolute power—one ring to rule them all—is alluring.

Most worshippers think only God is *truly* almighty, however. Earthly leaders are powerful but less than divine. Human monarchs have a measure of control, goes the logic, but the divine Monarch has immeasurably more. This form of omnipotence, the ability to secure outcomes singlehandedly, is considered the greatest power conceivable. The omnipotent One requires no help.

---

24. Schmitt, *Political Theology*, 10. For an examination of God and the laws of nature, see Jeffrey Koperski, *Divine Action, Determinism, and the Laws of Nature* (Routledge, 2022).

25. Joerg Reiger shows how this view affects God's relation to economics. "The classical theist notion of omnipotence, which has no real match in the Bible if perceived as an absolute topdown category, has been revitalized by the top-down flow of money in the free-market economy," Reiger argues. See *No Rising Tide* (Minneapolis, Mn.: Fortress, 2009), 80.

26. John Sanders explores the consequences of thinking God is authoritarian or nurturant in *Embracing Prodigals* (Eugene, Or.: Wipf and Stock, 2020).

Omnipotence Endorses Politics

The problem is not only that humans project onto God the desire for control that they find among earthly leaders. An omnipotent Divine King also directly or indirectly legitimizes the rule of earthly kings. A controlling God ordains the authority of presidents, lords, prime ministers, CEOs, managers, and anyone else in power, whether they were elected or installed by fiat or with violence. After all, an all-powerful Being can on a whim install, prevent, permit, or overthrow anyone.

Some point to biblical passages as support for the claim that God picks political leaders and systems. "Let every person be subordinate to the higher authorities," the Apostle Paul tells readers in Rome, "for there is no authority except from God, and those that exist have been established by God. Whoever resists authority opposes what God has appointed, and those who oppose it will bring judgment upon themselves" (Rom. 13:1-2). Adolf Hitler realized the benefits of this argument, and he was fond of calling God, "The Almighty."[27]

When believers agree with those in power, Paul's words provide evidence God also agrees. The ruler is divinely sanctioned. They ignore Jesus when he says, "the kings of the Gentiles lord it over them . . . but not so with you" (Lk. 22:25-26). When believers don't like a leader or political system, they appeal to other biblical passages that justify opposition to earthly authorities.

Some leaders capitalize on the implications of omnipotence by invoking God as the basis of their authority. This brings disastrous results. One of the more notorious is the so-called "Doctrine of Discovery," issued by Pope Nicholas V to King Alfonso of Portugal. Here, the Pope sanctions the "discovering" and colonizing of lands and the subjugation of Indigenous

---

27. Karl Barth, *Dogmatics in Outline*, G. T. Thompson, trans. (New York: Harper, 1959), 48.

people, including "reducing their persons to perpetual slavery." He issued this decree "by the authority of Almighty God conferred upon us," and says we should trust "in Him from whom empires and governments and all good things proceed." He warns that no one "infringe" or "contravene" his permission, else that person "incur the wrath of Almighty God."[28] Because so many have invoked an omnipotent God to justify their oppression of others, postcolonial and liberation theologians today are rethinking divine providence.[29]

More recently, Evangelical Christians claimed an omnipotent God appointed Donald Trump as President of the United States. Trump aligned himself with Evangelicals because doing so secured votes for his campaign and support for his policies. Doing so also granted Trump, in the minds of some, divine authority. The logic of omnipotence leads naturally to thinking God puts leaders in power, so it's not surprising Evangelicals would say God put Trump in the White House. What should surprise us is when other Christians accept omnipotence but criticize Evangelicals when they follow its logic.

A common retort to this argument says God differs in a crucial way from human rulers: God is perfectly *good*. Human leaders are not. "There are no absolutely good people," say some, "but we worship an absolutely Good and Omnipotent King."[30] God is a Benevolent Dictator. To put it another way, controlling tyrants cause harm, but controlling Love does not.

---

28. Pope Alexander VI's Demarcation Bull, May 4, 1493. Also known as "The Doctrine of Discovery." https://www.gilderlehrman.org/history-resources/spotlight-primary-source/doctrine-discovery-1493 (Accessed 1/6/22)

29. For example, see Ekaputra Tupamahu, "A Decolonial View of God," in *Uncontrolling Love*, Lisa Michaels, et. al., eds (Grasmere, Id.: SacraSage, 2017) and Randy S. Woodley, *Indigenous Theology and the Western Worldview: A Decolonialized Approach to Christian Doctrine* (Grand Rapids, Mich.: Baker, 2022).

30. Jonathan Foster portrays controlling divine power as "Omnipotence" with a capital O. See his *Theology of Consent: Mimetic Theory in an Open and Relational Universe* (Grasmere, Id.: SacraSage, 2022).

This argument falters for many reasons, but I'll mention two. First, it ignores our first-hand experience as agents with power and freedom.[31] If omnipotence means God exerts all power or controls others, God cannot be omnipotent and creatures have power and freedom. And if benevolence is always persuasive, "Benevolent Dictator" is a contradiction. Dictators don't persuade, they control.

Second, when pointless pain and unnecessary suffering occur, believers rightly wonder why an allegedly good and omnipotent King does not stop them. The Benevolent Dictator must be asleep. Claiming an all-powerful God differs from powerful kings by being consistently good fails to align with our experience of genuine evil. A benevolent being who *can* stop evil *does* stop it.

To worship God as omnipotent, therefore, is explicitly or implicitly to endorse the ruler or political system of the day.

Most worshippers will not admit to this endorsement, of course. Tyrants may demand sovereignty, but most believers would not say God sanctions a tyrant's abuse. However, believing God can do absolutely anything, control others, or has all power means God *wants* whatever leader or system is in power. At least God wants them more than wanting someone or something else. Omnipotence can make political changes in an instant.

John Calvin identifies the folly in thinking there's an ultimate difference between an omnipotent God permitting oppressive authorities or policies and God willing them. We should make "no distinction between God's will and God's permission," says Calvin. "Why shall we say 'permission' unless it is because God so wills?"[32] In another writing, Calvin

---

31. Among books arguing for the irreducibility of freedom, see Jeffrey F. Keuss, *Freedom of the Self* (Pickwick, 2010); Timothy O'Connor, *Persons and Causes* (Oxford, 2002).

32. John Calvin, *Institutes of the Christian Religion*, John T. McNeill, ed., Ford Lewis Battles, trans. (Philadelphia: Westminster, 1960), III.23.8.

puts it bluntly: "What else is the permission of Him who has the power of preventing and in whose hand the whole matter is placed but his will?"[33]

Saying an omnipotent God *permits* tyrants and tyranny is no different from saying God *wants* them.

And Yet . . .

And yet . . .

Sometimes worshiping God as King of kings and Lord of lords functions as a prophetic cry *against* ruling authorities and systems of oppression. Writers of scripture and believers throughout history have appealed to God when *opposing* whichever Caesar of the day terrorizes or political order denies them dignity. Citing allegiance to a Divine Lord, many *reject* earthly politicians and social arrangements that destroy. "God before king," they say. "The kingdom of heaven differs from the kingdoms of this age."

This is the primary reason biblical authors call God *sabaoth* in the Hebrew Bible and *pantokrator* in the New Testament. The *true* King leads armies against imposters who oppress (e.g., Daniel 4). The *universal* ruler is greater than any human whose rule is localized (e.g., Rev. 17:14; 19:6). God governs *forever*; the reigns of tyrants and tyrannical systems are temporary. "Jesus is Lord!" say many Christians, "Caesar is not."

Is it reasonable, however, to believe God is "in control" but claim God does not want harmful structures and leaders? I don't think so. If an omnipotent God ordains the rulers of this world, then resisting them means resisting what God ordained.

Does it make sense to say God is all-powerful and all-loving but also say God *does not* want monarchs and managers that do evil?[34] I don't think

---

33. John Calvin, *Commentaries on the First Book of Moses Called Genesis*, vol. 1 (Christian Classics Ethereal Library, Grand Rapids, Mich.) http://www.ccel.org Accessed 1/10/2023.

34. Using the example of the Philippines, Karl Villarmea says the "basic feature and operation" of established labor relationships "correspond to the idea of sovereignty of God in

so. If an omnipotent God wants abusers in power, those who defy them oppose God's wishes.

I'm not the first to ask such questions. But my answers differ from the usual fare. The typical answers assume God is omnipotent and shift the blame for evil elsewhere. But after believers realize the inadequacy of explanations that appeal the fall of Adam and Eve, God-allowed sin and rebellion, recalcitrant human nature, Satan, or the harmful vestiges of evolutionary history, many admit it's impossible to reconcile the omnipotent God they worship with the tyranny they endure.

Then, typically, out comes the mystery card: "God's ways are not our ways." "Finite creatures can't understand an infinite God." Or as Calvin put it, "In a wonderful and ineffable way, nothing happens contrary to [God's] will, even that which is contrary to his will!"[35] When faced with paradox, many people appeal to mystery rather than reconsider whatever beliefs create the inconsistency.

I have little doubt that humans—at least most of them—are worshiping creatures. And what we worship shapes how we see the world and who we become. Worship matters.[36] But worshiping God as omnipotent leads to confusion and despair.

If we praise God as an all-powerful rescuer, we rightly lose faith when we're not rescued.

---

classical theology." Karl James E. Villarmea, "Transcendence in the Time of Neoliberalism," in *Faith, Class, and Labor: Intersectional Approaches in a Global Context*, Jin Young Choi and Joerg Rieger, eds. (Eugene, OR: Pickwick, 2020), 236. Joerg Reiger addresses issues of power and class in *Theology in the Capitalocene* (Minneapolis, Mn.: Fortress, 2022).

35. John Calvin, *The Secret Providence of God*, 81.

36. Keith Ward is among many who claim humans are, by nature, worshipers. See *Religion and Human Nature* (Oxford: Oxford University Press, 1998). James K. A. Smith makes a powerful argument for the importance of worship in *Desiring the Kingdom: Worship, Worldview, and Cultural Formation* (Grand Rapids, Mich.: Baker, 2009).

Other Reasons to Stop Believing God Exists

The experience of evil leads millions to unbelief and most believers to bewilderment. Worshipping God as omnipotent implicates the Almighty as either causing or permitting horrendous events and unnecessary suffering. An omnipotent God is guilty.

Belief in omnipotence leads to other reasons many people stop believing God exists. As I argued above, it implies that God appoints and upholds political leaders and policies. A God capable of control could replace tyrants and erase tyranny singlehandedly. Yet political oppression persists. If we follow the logic of omnipotence, we should presume this oppression is God's will. Although worshiping God as their *true* Leader inspires some to resist, few believers realize they can follow a Divine Leader but reject omnipotence.

Omnipotence also supports the false claim that the Bible is inerrant. A loving God would apparently want a crystal-clear revelation of what's necessary for salvation. The Almighty could also guarantee the writing and safekeeping of that revelation. So it's not surprising when Fundamentalists insist the Bible is inerrant, despite it being far from error-free. They simply follow the logic of omnipotence and then try to explain away scriptural inconsistencies. They also declare, "The Bible clearly says," assuming God guarantees their interpretations as valid. Omnipotence supports believing the Bible is infallible and unambiguous.

Omnipotence is necessary for the traditional view of hell. It requires controlling power to send people against their will to conscious torment and everlastingly keep them there. Only an all-powerful God can detain the damned in misery forever. Because belief in hell so obviously conflicts with the claim that God loves everyone, the absurdity leads many to reject faith altogether.[37]

---

37. I explain this in "Relentless Love as God's Glory," in *Deconstructing Hell*, Chad Bahl, ed. (Grasmere, Id.: SacraSage, 2023). Other essays in this volume also reject hell.

Or take evolution and the billions-of-years-old universe. I have yet to meet a young-earth creationist who denies omnipotence. Of course, one can embrace science in general and evolution in particular while also believing God is all-powerful. But an instant and flawless creation aligns with omnipotence better than a long evolutionary process, with its dead-ends, disorder, ugliness, and mass extinctions. Those who endorse evolutionary creation or theistic evolution are wise to reject omnipotence.

Omnipotence is assumed by those who think God alone decides gender and sexual orientation. An all-powerful God could create clear binaries. The old saw "God created Adam and Eve, not Adam and Steve" rests on the assumption an almighty Creator singlehandedly decided human nature. Yet the bodies and desires of LGBTQIA+ people attest to nonbinaries and non-heteronormativity. Giving up omnipotence makes it easier to account for gender and sexual diversity, because it means creaturely agency, chance, environment, genetics, experiences, and more contribute to our becoming who we are.

I conclude with a final obstacle created when believers worship God as omnipotent: the absence of profound religious experiences for certain people. Although some worshippers testify to intense encounters with the divine, others do not. God is hidden. One would think a loving God would want dramatic experiences for all who seek them, and an omnipotent God could guarantee they occur. It's understandable, therefore, why those who are frustrated by their lack of religious experiences come to doubt God exists at all.[38]

Worshipping God as omnipotent generates immense harm and, for some, unbelief.

---

38. Brian McLaren addresses many of these issues in his work. See, for instance, *Faith After Doubt* (New York: St. Martins, 2021). See also Mark Karris, *Religious Refugees* (Quoir, 2020).

Solving the Problem of Evil

What if God exists but is *not* omnipotent?

What if God *can't* stop evil singlehandedly? What if God does not cause or even allow suffering, because God *does not* have all power? What if God is not "in control" and, in fact, *can't* control anyone or anything?

What if God does not appoint political leaders or systems, cannot prevent biblical errors or guarantee perfect interpretations, sends no one to hell, cannot instantly create complex life or guarantee perfect design, does not singlehandedly decide sexual orientations and gender identity, and cannot guarantee everyone enjoys profound religious experiences?

In the remainder of this chapter, I focus on the problem of evil. I offer a solution with six dimensions, each of which rejects omnipotence. I have explained this solution and its dimensions in previous books, but here I highlight problems omnipotence creates for traditional responses to evil.[39] Those responses are salvageable if we disconnect them from the idea God is all-powerful. I conclude by briefly explaining why rejecting omnipotence overcomes other obstacles to belief.

1. God can't prevent evil singlehandedly.

The strongest of the traditional responses to evil points to creaturely freedom. If God creates complex creatures, gives them freedom, and those creatures use that freedom wrongly, we should blame creatures for evil not God. Many call this the "free-will defense."

Those who embrace the free-will defense typically say God wants *real* relationships, which requires that humans have the genuine ability to cooperate with or reject divine overtures. God knows that the control

---

39. I explain in accessible prose my solution to the problem of evil in *God Can't*. For more academic explanations, see *The Uncontrolling Love of God* and *Pluriform Love*. See also Oord, "An Essential Kenosis Solution to the Problem of Evil," in Meister and Dew, eds., *God and the Problem of Evil*.

of people undermines the authenticity of their decision-making, so God rarely does so. After all, as William Hasker puts it, "frequent and routine interventions by God to prevent the misuse of freedom by creatures would undermine the structure of human life and community intended in the plan of creation."[40]

God also needed a package of creaturely processes as the environment for human freedom. Without a stable environment, human choosing would be impossible. So it's God's general policy rarely to interrupt the laws of nature or tweak the processes of creation. God seldom controls.

The free-will defense offers insights. But it fails as a full-fledged solution to the problem of evil. It does so for several reasons, and I'll mention two.

The first problem with the free-will defense pertains to exceptions for divine action made by most who embrace it. Those exceptions say God *usually* respects free will but occasionally does not. God *typically* gives freedom but may withhold it, depending on the circumstances. Sometimes God controls creatures or creation to do miracles, for instance. An omnipotent God can withdraw, override, or choose not to provide freedom or sustain natural laws. General policies allow for exceptions.

If God sometimes fiddles with freedom, however, victims and survivors rightly wonder if God loves them. They wonder why God does not withdraw, override, or retain the freedom used wrongly by their abusers. "If God can stop my brother from cussing," we ask, "why didn't God stop my rape?"

Most who embrace the free will defense claim an omnipotent God deliberately self-limits to allow creatures to act freely.[41] They say God "won't" or "doesn't" always stop evil. God "reserves the right to intervene, if

---

40. See William Hasker, "An Open Theist View," in *God and the Problem of Evil*.

41. Theologians have long explored the distinction between God's potential power and the actual expression of divine power. For a historical summery, see Richardson, "Meister Eckhart's Parisian Question."

necessary," says Jack Cottrell. "Thus he is able not only to *permit* human actions to occur, but also to *prevent* them from occurring if he so chooses."[42]

This implies, however, that God sometimes allows or permits evil. An omnipotent God could prevent the misery survivors endured, but chooses not to. If love prevents preventable evil, the God who chooses not to prevent evil isn't loving. A self-limited God can make exceptions to the usual practice of giving freedom and sustaining natural processes. If God is self-limited, therefore, victims and survivors despair. God doesn't care enough to stop their suffering.

The second problem with the free-will defense is its limited scope. Most free will theists think God gives freedom to humans and doesn't usually control them. But many think God controls lesser creatures, simpler organisms, and inanimate entities of nature. God also sustains but can suspend natural laws. In other words, God does or can control the nonhuman world and interrupt the laws of nature.

Believing God controls simpler beings and the natural laws means God is ultimately responsible for pandemics, disease, nonhuman predation, genetic mutation, and harm-causing quantum events. An omnipotent God can also manipulate the conditions of creation to eliminate harmful possibilities for free will creatures. Victims rightly wonder why this God doesn't alter circumstances or suspend natural laws to prevent their harm.[43] Apparently, this God isn't concerned.

In sum, the omnipotent God of the traditional free-will defense is culpable for failing to prevent evil.

The free-will defense makes more sense if we deny omnipotence. To solve the problem of evil, we should believe God *cannot* control any

---

42. Jack Cottrell, "The Nature of Divine Sovereignty," in *The Grace of God, the Will of Man*, ed. Clark H. Pinnock (Grand Rapids: Zondervan, 1989), 112.

43. For a concise summary of the issues of God's limitations in relation to omnipotence, see Hoffman and Rosenkrantz, "Omnipotence," in *A Companion to Philosophy of Religion*. See also Atle Ottesen Sovik, *The Problem of Evil and the Power of God* (Unipub AS, 2009).

creature, complex or simple. And God *cannot* suspend the law-like regularities of existence. If God cannot control creatures and creation—from free-will choosers to inanimate matter to the laws of nature—we rightly blame creatures who freely choose wrongly or random events that cause harm. The God who can't stop evil singlehandedly is not to blame.

Why can't God stop evil singlehandedly? Why is it impossible for God to control creatures and creation? I'll propose a reason in the final chapter. It builds upon the nature of God's love as uncontrolling. But the first and most crucial dimension to solving the problem of evil says God *can't* control creatures or creation.

God is not omnipotent.

2. God empathizes with our suffering.

To explore the second dimension of a solution to the problem of evil, let's return to Augustine. Not only does Augustine think God "can do all things," as he put it, he also believes God does not suffer. This means God cannot feel pain and is unaffected by the agony we endure.[44] The idea God that is unaffected and feels no emotional response is the classic view of divine impassibility.

Augustine links belief in impassibility to omnipotence. "[God] is called omnipotent on account of His doing what He wills, not on account of His suffering what He wills not; for if that should befall Him, He would by no means be omnipotent."[45] If suffering "should befall" God, says Augustine,

---

44. In antiquity, to "suffer" meant to be affected by something or someone. A person suffers when affected by events that bring joy or sadness, pleasure or pain. Today, to "suffer" is associated with negative emotions and pain. Because the ancient use covers but extends beyond the contemporary connotation, Augustine's use of "suffering" fits my arguments about divine omnipotence and suffering as experiencing pain.

45. Augustine, "Whether Our Wills are Ruled by Necessity," *City of God and Christian Doctrine*, ch 10. https://www.ccel.org/ccel/schaff/npnf102.iv.V.10.html (Accessed 1/11/23).

God would not be almighty. An all-powerful God, he argues, does not suffer or empathize with those in pain.[46]

Augustine's view of perfection and worries about change drive him to think God cannot empathize.[47] A perfect God would be in all ways unchanging, he thinks, but a God who emotionally responds will change from one emotional state to another. Because God is perfect, and a changing God cannot remain faithful, God never suffers. This means, however, that an omnipotent God feels no compassion for victims and survivors.[48] God doesn't care.

The second dimension in my six-fold solution to the problem of evil rejects Augustine's views of impassibility and omnipotence.[49] God *does* feel the pain of those harmed and hurting. God empathizes with us, responds emotionally to our pain, and experiences compassion. The nonomnipotent God that I propose is a "fellow-sufferer who understands," as Whitehead put it.[50] God cares.

The suffering God, however, is not overwhelmed nor incapacitated by suffering. Nor does feeling the negative effects of evil tempt God to be

---

46. Thomas Aquinas also thinks God is not affected by creatures. "A relation of God to creatures is not a reality in God," he writes. In this way of thinking, God knows creatures as ideas without being causally affected by them. Influencing relations with creation "are not really in Him," Aquinas says, and "are ascribed to him only in our understanding." In other words, we only *imagine* God gives and receives in loving relationship. See Thomas Aquinas, *Summa Theologica*; *Summa Contra Gentiles* II (Notre Dame: University of Notre Dame Press, 1981), 13-14.

47. I explain Augustine's views of perfection and impassibility in *Pluriform Love*, chs. 5-6. For another exploration of Augustine and love, see Werner Jeanrond, *A Theology of Love*.

48. See Roberto Sirvent for a strong argument for linking *imitatio dei* and divine passibility (*Embracing Vulnerability: Human and Divine* [Eugene, Or.: Pickwick, 2014]).

49. I address divine empathy and the problem of evil in *God Can't*, ch. 2. See also Edward Farley, *Divine Empathy* (Philadelphia: Fortress, 1996); Paul Fiddes, *The Creative Suffering of God* (Oxford: Oxford University Press, 1988); Jürgen Moltmann, *The Crucified God* (London: SCM, 1974); Jeff B. Pool, *God's Wounds: Hermeneutic of the Christian Symbol of Divine Suffering: Vol. 1 Divine Vulnerability and Creation* (Cambridge: James Clarke & Co., 2009); Anna Case-Winters, *God Will Be All in All: Theology Through the Lens of Incarnation* (Louisville, Ky.: Westminster John Knox, 2021).

50. Alfred North Whitehead, *Process and Reality*, 351.

wicked. Although the divine experience changes moment by moment as God feels the joys and sorrows of others, the divine nature is unaffected and never changes. The God whose unchanging essence is love will *never* do evil. God can't. But the God whose changing experience loves moment by moment does suffer with sufferers. God can. I call this idea God's "essence-experience binate," while others call it dipolar theism.[51] It overcomes Augustine's worries by saying God's loving experience changes, but God's loving essence does not.

An increasing number of theologians embrace the idea that God suffers when creatures suffer. Relational theology is on the rise.[52] Many who embrace divine empathy, however, retain belief in omnipotence. God is both relational and all-powerful, they say, God grieves but is in control. Some even appeal to a suffering God to solve the problem of evil.

Believing God empathizes with suffering does not, in itself, solve the problem of evil. The God who could stop pointless pain but chooses instead to suffer with victims is not loving. Love prevents preventable evil. A loving person does not allow pointless pain if they can stop it. Consequently, a relational but all-powerful God is guilty of failing to prevent evil. Saying God empathizes with creaturely suffering must be supplemented with saying God is not omnipotent.

In *The Cross and the Lynching Tree*, James Cone uses documents, stories, and anecdotes to show why Black Christians in America believe that God—revealed in Jesus—suffers with those who suffer. "Black ministers

---

51. For an accessible explanation of God's essence-experience binate, see *Open and Relational Theology*, 102-03. Charles Hartshorne raised the phrase "dipolar theism" to prominence. See his essay "The Dipolar Conception of Deity," *Review of Metaphysics* 21:2 [1967], 273-89) and Donald Viney's explanation in "Hartshorne's Dipolar Theism and the Mystery of God" *Philosophia*, 35 (2007), 341-350. For good explorations of Hartshorne's theological views, see Daniel Dombrowski, *Analytic Theism, Hartshorne, and the Concept of God*; Donald Wayne Viney and George W. Shields, *The Mind of Charles Hartshorne* (Anoka, Mn.: Process Century, 2020).

52. The Center for Open and Relational Theology provides excellent resources for relational thinking. See c4ort.com.

preached about Jesus' death more than any other theme," says Cone, "because they saw in Jesus' suffering and persecution a parallel to their own encounter with slavery, segregation, and the lynching tree."[53] Cone does *not* say, however, that Jesus' death resolves questions about God and evil. "If God loves Black people," he asks, "why then do we suffer so much? That was my question as a child; that is still my question."[54]

In *Making a Way Out of No Way*, Monica Coleman also says making sense of suffering—especially the abuse of Black women and LGBTQ people—requires a suffering God. But Coleman rejects omnipotence. "God's power is persuasive," she writes. "God cannot make us do one thing or another. Rather, God influences, persuades, lures, or 'calls' us to embrace the principles of God's vision in every context."[55] This means "the quest for health and healing in the midst of violence, oppression, and evil is a lifelong cooperative process between God and us."[56] Rejecting omnipotence while affirming divine suffering allows Coleman to answer Cone's question.

An empathetic but not omnipotent God feels our pain but did not cause or permit it.

3. God works to heal.

The third dimension of my solution to the problem of evil addresses healing. Rather than wonder why evil happens, some wonder if victims and

---

53. James H. Cone, *The Cross and the Lynching Tree* (Maryknoll, NY: Orbis, 2011), 75.

54. Ibid., 154. In his earlier book, *God of the Oppressed* (London: SPCK, 1977), Cone argues that Black theology cannot give up omnipotence. This leads, of course, to Cone being unable to solve the problem of God's love and lynching. He overstates the commitment of Black theologians to omnipotence, however, because other Black theologians reject it. On this issue, see David P. Polk, *God of Empowering Love* (Anoka, Mn.: Process Century, 2016), ch. 15.

55. Monica A. Coleman, *Making a Way Out of No Way: A Womanist Theology* (Minneapolis, Mn.: Fortress, 2008), 59.

56. Ibid., 169. See also Coleman's handbook for congregational response to sexual violence, *The Dinah Project* (Eugene, OR.: Wipf and Stock, 2004).

survivors will heal. For them, the question is less about why evil occurs and more about whether its effects will be overcome. God must be omnipotent, say some, if we hope to get better.[57]

Questions about healing often coincide with questions about miracles. Those who heal slowly, through traditional medicines, or because of trained physicians, are unlikely to call their restoration miraculous. But those healed instantly often claim to have experienced the miraculous work of an omnipotent God. In fact, miracles are considered by many to be supernatural events God alone does.[58]

The problems with claims about supernatural miracles are obvious to those who reflect on them. If God heals some, why not all? If God does miracles sometimes, why not more often? And because instant healings are rare, why should we think they're divine actions? Perhaps it's blind luck.

In their study *Religion and AIDS in Africa*, Jenny Trinitapoli and Alexander Weinreb note the connection between thinking God is omnipotent and claiming God heals miraculously. This connection unfortunately leads few African Christians to seek cures for AIDS victims. "They merely articulate a deeply held theological principle that an omnipotent God can heal any illness," report the authors. But the fact that such healings "are seldom observed plays directly into [Christian] interpretations of AIDS as divine punishment."[59] Because an omnipotent God can heal but rarely does, God must *want* AIDS as punishment.

---

57. I address questions of healing in *God Can't*, ch. 3 and *Questions and Answers for God Can't*, ch. 2-3. See also Bruce Epperly, *Praying with Process Theology* (River Lane, 2017); and Ryan Lambros, *Eumorphosis: A Process-Relational Framework for Healing* (Doctoral Dissertation at Northwind Theological Seminary, 2023).

58. I address the problem with defining miracles as supernatural, then define miracles differently and defend that definition in *The Uncontrolling Love of God*, ch. 8.

59. Jenny Trinitapoli and Alexander Weinreb, *Religion and AIDS in Africa* (Oxford: Oxford University Press, 2012), 149.

These issues raise what I call "the problem of selective healing."[60] It's true that people sometimes heal. Most do so through natural processes or because of modern medicine. But occasionally someone heals quickly or unexpectedly. If we think an omnipotent God instantly heals some but not others, we face the problem of selective miracles. Why are some restored quickly, others slowly, and many not at all? Does God choose—select— some but allow most to suffer or die?

Rather than seek plausible answers to these questions, many believers play the mystery card. "God's ways are not our ways." Or "God has a plan that's beyond our ken." And "Just have faith!"

Giving up omnipotence overcomes the problem of selective healing. God so conceived works to heal *all* who hurt from accidents, disease, self-harm, abuse, or injustice. But healing *always* requires creaturely cooperation or the alignment of conditions in creation. It *never* comes through divine control. Healing requires the uncontrolling love of the Great Physician and creaturely cooperation or conducive conditions.

Notice the phrase "works to heal" in this dimension of my solution. I use it to indicate the necessary role God plays, whether healing comes slowly or quickly, predictably or unexpectedly. "Works to heal" means God can't heal singlehandedly but operates alongside creaturely actors, forces, and factors. Recover varies in speed or may not come at all, but it's not solely determined by God. Divine healing requires cooperation from creatures, their cells, muscles, organs, or components of their bodies. Or it requires conducive conditions among inanimate creation. Or healing depends upon relationships or social arrangements. God cannot heal alone.

Saying divine healing requires creaturely cooperation or conducive conditions does not mean we should blame victims when they do not heal. Nor does a lack of healing come from a lack of faith, at least in most cases. Our bodies sometimes do not cooperate with God, even when our

---

60. I address and explain the problem of selective healing in *God Can't*, ch. 3.

minds do. Sometimes the general conditions of creation are not aligned with God's wishes, even if we are. Sometimes we collaborate with God's healing work, but our communities do not. Despite our willingness, other forces, factors, and actors can thwart the healing God desires.

Healings and miracles, as well as their absence, make sense if God works to heal but is not omnipotent.

4. God works to squeeze good from bad.

It's common for scholars and everyday people to claim evil is necessary for good.[61] "God is teaching you a lesson," some say to suffering people. "This pain will make you stronger," say others. These answers align with what scholars call "soul-making" theodicies. According to them, God allows or causes pain and suffering for our benefit: to bring souls to maturity, to build character, or to educate us. What we consider evil is necessary for some personal good.

Other versions of this answer operate from a big picture perspective. They say evils are necessary for greater good. From a God's-eye view, goes the argument, our struggles play a role in all things working together for good (Rm. 8:28). This means, of course, that all pain and suffering must not be *genuinely* evil. Or, as Augustine puts it, "to [God] there is nothing at all evil," because horrors and holocausts "harmonize" to make a beautiful whole.[62]

Personal good and greater good theodicies agree that the world is better off, all things considered, because an omnipotent God caused or allowed events we consider evil. We may not understand this. But we should trust that all pain and suffering are good for us or the world.

This response to suffering, although profoundly inadequate, contains two truths. The first is that pain and suffering sometimes brings good.

---

61. I address this issue in *God Can't*, ch. 4.
62. Augustine, *Confessions*, VII, 13.

We sometimes learn from what we endure, and sometimes the suffering of a few secures good for others. We may look back on former troubles and believe that without them, some present benefit would not have been possible. And we may be right. "If he had never cheated," we might say of a former lover, "I would have missed out on you."

As typically described, this response is inadequate because it says *all* painful events bring personal or greater goods. This is not true. Victims of rape and torture are not better off, for instance. Child abuse and sex trafficking are not, overall, a net gain. Genocides don't make the world a better place. Sometimes the world grows more ill instead of healthier, and rather than get better, people grow bitter. Others lose faith.

While good sometimes comes from suffering, not *all* suffering brings greater good.

The second truth in this traditional but inadequate response to evil says humans have a limited perspective. We "see through a glass darkly," to quote the Apostle Paul, and we are not omniscient (1 Cor. 13:12). Good theology acknowledges limits to human knowledge. Any proposed solution to the problem of evil, including mine, should be tentative, speculative, and provisional. Because complete understanding is not possible for mere mortals, we should not claim to be certain about such matters.

Given our lack of certainty and limited perspectives, it's tempting to think there are no grounds to believe any event is evil. We can't see the whole picture, after all, or know what's best in the long run. Perhaps what we *think* makes us or the world worse actually improves both. Only an omniscient and everlasting Observer could judge.

Often missed in this argument is that claims about limited knowledge and lack of certainty cut both ways. Those who say evil might be good from God's perspective rarely acknowledge the opposite: what we think is good may be evil. Our praise and thanks for God's good provisions, therefore, may be misguided. Given our flawed judgement, God may be doing evil. Why should we consider *any* actions loving—divine or creaturely—if our judgements cannot be trusted? The truth is that we all believe evils occur that make us and the world worse. In fact, we *act* and *feel* as if genuine evils occur. Our feelings of regret, guilt, moral outrage, remorse, or indignation reveal that we sometimes think life could have been better, all things considered. And we act accordingly. We all *live* as if evil is real.

I call this an "experiential nonnegotiable."[63] In our lived experience, we all acknowledge that some events cause pointless pain. This deeply lived reality can be denied in conversation but not in practice. The fact that evil occurs is a basic belief that we inevitably presuppose. Because good theology must account for basic beliefs and lived realities, it must account for evil. We're experiential hypocrites if we say everything makes the world better.

The fourth dimension to my solution to the problem of evil accounts for these truths. It admits that sometimes pain and suffering make things better overall. But it also acknowledges that sometimes genuine evils occur, and we and the world are worse because of them. Evil is real.

This dimension to the solution says a good God doesn't want unnecessary suffering and pointless pain. Because God is not omnipotent, however, God cannot stop pain and suffering by fiat. God can't. God doesn't give up or abandon us when evil happens, however. God works to squeeze whatever good can be squeezed from the bad God didn't want in the first place. God redeems.

The traditional soul-building and greater good theodicies can be salvaged if we detach them from omnipotence. Doing so means we don't have

---

63. David Ray Griffin calls these truths "hard-core commonsense notions." See his *Unsnarling the World-Knot: Consciousness, Freedom, and the Mind-Body Problem* (Berkeley: University of California Press, 1998), 34, 210. Jürgen Habermas calls them "performative contradictions." See his "Discourse Ethics: Notes on a Program of Philosophical Justification," in *Moral Consciousness and Communicative Action*, trans. C. Lenhardt and S.W. Nicholsen (Cambridge, Mass.: MIT Press, 1990).

to believe "everything happens for a reason."[64] Genuine evil isn't part of some foreknown plan designed to build our characters or make the world better. God does not permit evil in order to teach us lessons or get us to repent.

Instead, God tries to produce something positive from the negative God didn't want when it happened. God works with whatever occurs and with all of creation to bring something beautiful from what is ugly, something healthy from what is sick, and something good from evil. Some things are not possible, and growth is not inevitable, but something good may emerge.

The God who is not omnipotent works to promote growth in the aftermath of evil.

5. God needs creaturely cooperation.

Some believers claim God invites us to participate in the work of salvation. We have a role to play in overcoming evil with good. Coming together in communities of care is often central to this process. We should express acts of love and develop habits that support well-being. As we participate with God, we can be God's "fellow workers" (1 Cor. 3:9).

In his book, *God, Medicine and Suffering,* Stanley Hauerwas makes this argument. But he also says it's unnecessary to solve the problem of evil. "Apparently it never occurred to the early Christians to question their belief in God or even God's goodness because they were unjustly suffering for their beliefs," says Hauerwas. "Rather, their faith gave them direction in the face of persecution and general misfortune." For them, "suffering was not a metaphysical problem needing a solution but a practical challenge requiring a response."[65]

---

64. For a popular criticism of the idea that everything happens for a reason, see Kate Bowler, *Everything Happens for a Reason . . . and Other Lies I've Loved* (New York: Random House, 2018).

65. Stanley Hauerwas, *God, Medicine and Suffering (Grand Rapids, Mich.: Eerdmans, 1994),* 53.

Hauerwas seems to ignore wide swaths of scripture when making these claims, especially biblical passages of lament and questioning, as well as passages about metaphysical forces and evil actors.[66] But his main point is that believers should work against evil rather than try to figure out why God causes or allows it.

Like most who call us to work against evil, Hauerwas affirms omnipotence.[67] But this affirmation undercuts a believer's motivation to alleviate suffering. After all, an omnipotent God can fix any problem without our help. This God might choose to include our efforts, but the Almighty doesn't *need* us. We're superfluous.

An omnipotent God causes or allows *all* ills and ails. And if God causes or allows these evils, the Almighty must *want* them . . . at least more than the alternatives. Those who work against unnecessary suffering apparently oppose God's wishes. If God is loving, wise, and all-powerful, after all, God must orchestrate everything for a purpose.

If an omnipotent God allows injustice, why march against it? It must be God's plan. If an omnipotent God permits starvation, why feed the hungry? If an all-powerful deity turns a blind eye to racism, genocide, climate change, and more, why should we care about those problems? Why try to improve our lives if an almighty God wills this mess?

These questions point out contradictions that arise from believing God is omnipotent. They also fit John Calvin's irrational thinking. I'll quote him again: "Nothing happens contrary to [God's] will, even that which is contrary to his will."[68] If we delete the double negatives in this sentence, we find Calvin saying *everything* is the will of an omnipotent God, whether God causes or allows it.

---

66. For an argument that accounts for spiritual warfare and the problem of evil, see Gregory Boyd, *Satan and the Problem of Evil* (IVP, 2001).

67. See Stanley Hauerwas, *Approaching the End: Eschatological Reflections on Church, Politics, and Life* (Grand Rapids, Mich.: Eerdmans, 2013).

68. John Calvin, *The Secret Providence of God*, 81.

Everything *does* happen for a reason if God is omnipotent.

To make sense of "God invites our participation to work against suffering," we must reject omnipotence and believe God needs us. The fifth dimension of a solution to evil says God *needs* creatures in the work of overcoming evil with good. The uncontrolling Lover requires the beloved's responses in the work to save the world. The Creator-creature love synergy is indispensable because both Creator and creatures are indispensable for prevailing against evil.[69] God needs us.

To say God needs creation does not mean creatures alone stop evil. It's not all on us. While God can't prevent evil singlehandedly, creatures can't prevent it without help. For love to win, a loving Creator needs creation's loving responses, and creatures need their Creator's empowering love.[70] That's how love works.

The cooperation dimension to the problem of evil returns us to an issue we addressed in the previous chapter: God's incorporeality. We noted that creatures sometimes use their bodies to prevent evil. A mother might grab a child the instant before a car hits it, for instance. A hen might put herself between her chicks and a snake. A firefighter might pull an elderly patient from a burning building. These loving actions are not instances of control, in the sense of the rescuers being the *only* (sufficient) causes. But the impact of these embodied creatures allows them to do activities a bodiless God cannot.

Claiming God is an incorporeal spirit explains why God can't stop the evils that embodied creatures sometimes can. It also identifies crucial reasons why God *needs* us. Sometimes to rescue, a loving God requires creaturely bodies cooperating with divine desires. Often the liberation,

---

69. I explain indispensable love synergy in *God Can't*, ch. 5.

70. On transformation, see Sheri D. Kling, *A Process Spirituality* (London: Rowman and Littlefield, 2020). On God's empowering love, see Polk, *God of Empowering Love* and Joshua D. Reichard, "Relational Empowerment: A Process-Relational Theology of the Spirit-filled Life," *Pneuma: The Journal of the Society for Pentecostal Studies* 36, no. 2 (2014): 1-20.

protection, and salvation God yearns for demands the cooperation of embodied beings. Again, God needs us.

To overcome evil, a bodiless God, who is not omnipotent, needs our embodied cooperation.

6. God doesn't create from nothing.

The final dimension to a six-fold solution to evil addresses God's creating. It explains why evil events are possible in the first place and why God doesn't create obstacles in the present to prevent them. A theology of God's creating matters for understanding evil.

It stands to reason that an omnipotent God who allegedly created the world out of nothing is solely responsible for all natural processes and creaturely freedom. At least at the beginning, no one and nothing contributed to the creative process. Presumably, an omnipotent God who creates from nothing can interrupt and interfere at any time in the history of that creation. This God could create something from nothing now, if so inclined. Omnipotence combined with creating-something-from-nothing abilities grants God absolute control and unchecked creativity.

The idea God that can or ever could create from nothing—creatio ex nihilo—presents obstacles to a theology that champions love.[71] The chief obstacle is its implications for evil. A God who created the universe from nothing is singly responsible for the fundamental creatures, laws, and structures of existence.

---

71. I explore this doctrine's problems for a coherent theology of love in *Pluriform Love*, ch. 8. See also Thomas Jay Oord, "Eternal Creation and Essential Love," in *T&T Handbook on Suffering and the Problem of Evil,* Johannes Grossel and Matthias Grebe, eds. (London: T&T Clark, 2022). In addition, creation from nothing entails the following five problems: (1) Absolute nothingness cannot be conceived. (2) The view was first proposed by Gnostics who assumed creation is inherently evil. (3) We have no evidence our universe originally came into being from nothing. (4) We have no evidence creatures or creaturely entities can emerge instantaneously at any time from absolute nothingness. (5) The view assumes God once acted all alone, but power is a social concept only meaningful in relation to others.

Victims and survivors wonder, however, why an omnipotent God who created *ex nihilo didn't* make a universe with *no* evil. Or at least a lot less. And they wonder why this God doesn't create impediments to evil in the present.[72] An all-powerful who once created from nothing would be able, instantly, to create something from nothing today. Alvin Plantinga advocates this view: "There is nothing to prevent God from . . . creating *ex nihilo* a full-grown horse in the middle of Times Square." An omnipotent God can do so, Plantinga adds, "without violating the principle of conservation of energy."[73]

If God can create from nothing, one wonders why the Almighty doesn't prevent the evils we endure.[74] Why doesn't God create stone walls between rapists and their victims? Or an antidote to cancer? Why not create obstacles between bullets and human targets? Why doesn't God instantly create a cure anytime a virus wreaks havoc? Or create weather conditions that prevent Putin's tanks from killing Ukrainians? Once we start imagining the ways God could stop evil by creating something from nothing, the problem of evil grows exponentially!

Plantinga and others think God foreknows all that will occur in the world God creates. This naturally leads victims to ask why the Almighty didn't choose a world without their pain and with less evil overall. The answer typically is that God creates the best of all possible worlds. But if our world is the best possible one, *every* evil we experience is necessary. Things can't be better. This means the rape, torture, disease, holocausts,

---

72. Yujin Nagasawa calls this problem the "argument from the imperfection of the actual world." See *Maximal God*, 87.

73. Alvin Plantinga, *Where the Conflict Really Lies: Science, Religion, and Naturalism* (Oxford: Oxford University Press, 2011), 78-79.

74. David Ray Griffin has argued this point in many publications, including "Creation out of Nothing, Creation out of Chaos, and the Problem of Evil," in *Encountering Evil*, and *Evil Revisited: Responses and Reconsiderations* (Albany, NY: SUNY, 1991).

and horrors we witness are *not* genuinely evil, because they don't make the world worse than it might have been.[75]

Conundrums like this induce appeals to mystery. In some unknown way, say advocates of this view, what we consider evil is actually good. Although we can't understand it, the horrors of this world are necessary. It's *all* good, including abuse, brutality, torment, and cruelty.

The way we all live our lives, however, indicates we don't really believe this. We don't act like *everything* is good. We live believing the world could have been better, and history didn't have to be exactly like it is. This isn't the best of all possible worlds.

The sixth dimension of my solution to the problem of evil rejects creation from nothing. It says God always—everlastingly—creates in each moment out of and alongside what God created previously. It's God's nature to create from something and never to create from nothing. Just as God had no absolute beginning, God's creating had no absolute beginning.

The God who always creates out of or alongside what God previously created doesn't singlehandedly decide the fundamental laws of existence. The possibilities for good and evil are inherent in the creaturely order; they're baked into what it means to be a creature or creation. God did not create the possibilities for evil; they arise naturally from the self-causation each creature expresses. And God cannot create impediments to evil today from nothing because creating something from nothing is never possible.

The denial of *creatio ex nihilo* begs for a replacement doctrine of creation. I've offered one that says God everlastingly and necessarily creates, loves, and invites creatures to respond. Because God always and lovingly

---

75. Hoffman and Rosenkrantz note this problem pertaining to best possible worlds scenarios in "Omnipotence," in *A Companion to Philosophy of Religion*, 234. A. J. Freddoso illustrates the problem and endorses the best of all possible worlds notion connected to Molinism. "God, the divine artisan, freely and knowingly plans, orders, and provides for all the effects that constitute His artefact, the created universe with its entire history, and executes His chosen plan by playing an active cause role sufficient to ensure its exact realization . . . Thus, whatever occurs is properly said to be specifically decreed by God." Freddoso, ed., *One Divine Foreknowledge* (Ithaca, N.Y.: Cornell University Press, 1988), 3.

creates in relation to what God previously created, I call my alternative *creatio ex creatione sempiternalis en amore.* Although God's creating had no absolute beginning, God initiates each moment of existence by creating alongside or out of what was previously created.[76]

Our Creator does not create from nothing, does not create evil, and is not omnipotent.

Overcoming Other Reasons

Earlier I noted obstacles to belief in God that is grounded in omnipotence. To clarify how these obstacles can be overcome when we stop believing God is all-powerful, I return to them.

If God exists but is not omnipotent, we don't need to believe God installs or supports all political leaders and policies. The God who is not all-powerful cannot singlehandedly overthrow tyrants and eliminate systemic tyranny. God cares about social arrangements and leaders, and God influences political processes by calling us to do what, given the circumstances, promotes the common good. But those calls can be ignored or misunderstood. And rejecting omnipotence fits our urge to resist rulers and systems that oppress.

The Bible makes better sense if God exists but is not omnipotent. We can believe it contains eternal truths without thinking God revealed those truths in an inerrant and crystal-clear way.[77] An uncontrolling God of

---

76. I lay out my alternative creation doctrine in *Pluriform Love*, ch. 8. See also Thomas Jay Oord, "Eternal Creation and Essential Love" in *T&T Handbook on Suffering and the Problem of Evil.* Mary-Jane Rubenstein provides scientific and philosophical groundwork for my position in *Worlds Without End* (New York: Columbia University Press, 2014). My view also aligns well with the tehomic theology of Catherine Keller. See *The Face of the Deep* (New York: Routledge, 2003).

77. On inspiration and uncontrolling love in biblical inspiration, see Gabriel Gordon, *God Speaks: A Participatory Theology of Inspiration* (Glen Oak, Ca.: Quoir, 2021); on inerrancy, see Gregory Boyd, *Inspired Imperfection* (Minneapolis: Fortress, 2020); and essays in Thomas Jay Oord and Richard Thompson, eds., *Rethinking the Bible* (Grasmere, ID: SacraSage, 2018).

love *always* communicates but *cannot* do so unambiguously nor guarantee infallible texts. Our interpretations of scripture will also vary, partly because God can't control our interpreting work. In other words, theories of biblical inspiration and interpretation that reject omnipotence better fit the Bible and our diverse interpretations.[78]

The logic of hell crumbles if we believe God is loving but not omnipotent. A loving God *would not* send anyone to eternal conscious torment, and a God who cannot control *could not* send anyone. Whatever conditions we encounter after death are not decided by God singlehandedly. Our future in this life and the next rests, in part, upon what we decide in response to a loving God and other creaturely decisions.

If God exists but is not omnipotent, leading theories of science make more sense. A God who cannot control did not create a young earth and cannot singlehandedly determine the evolutionary process. This God can't control brains and bodies nor manipulate cells and celestials. The non-omnipotent God cannot guarantee perfect design nor avert evolutionary dead-ends. We need not blame animal suffering, disorder, or ugliness upon the loving God who cannot control creatures or creation.[79] The influence and guidance of an active and loving God, however, is evident in the design and purpose we do find.

Gender and sexual diversity make better sense if God is not omnipotent. The variations in the bodies and desires of both LGBTQIA+ and straight and cisgender people fit a theology that says God works alongside creaturely agency, chance, environment, genetics, histories, and more.

---

78. Add to these arguments that an uncontrolling God could not guarantee the best results for the canonization process.

79. Bethany Sollereder addresses animal suffering and God's love in *God, Evolution, and Animal Suffering: Theodicy without a Fall* (New York: Routledge, 2020), as does Christopher Southgate, *The Groaning of Creation* (London: Westminster John Knox, 2008). Ilia Delio addresses love and evolution in *The Unbearable Wholeness of Being* (Maryknoll, NY: Orbis, 2013).

This God wants multifarious beauty and pluriform love.[80] Let a thousand, healthy flowers bloom.

If God exists but is not omnipotent, we better account for why some people enjoy profound religious experiences and others never do. A loving God does not voluntarily hide.[81] This God self-reveals—given the factors and actors at play—and invites all to transformative encounters. Some may not be aware of these invitations, some may be constitutionally blocked from them, and others may choose to avoid them. Still others may seek metaphysically impossible experiences, and they should not be surprised that the impossible is impossible. Because God is not omnipotent, there is no guarantee everyone will enjoy dramatic encounters with God they crave.

An omnipotent God does not exist; we have reasons to think an uncontrolling God does.

Conclusion

The problem of evil ends omnipotence. At least it should. When we realize omnipotence was not born in the Bible and philosophy qualifies it to death, the problem of evil should bury the corpse for good. Just as former beliefs that the earth is flat or that women are inferior are now dead to us, the belief in omnipotence should likewise be dead to us.

Omnipotence remains on life support due to high church liturgies and low church piety, which shape the theologies of countless people. Believers often consider God to be the King of kings and Lord of lords, and this praise can affect how they imagine God's role in politics. Many worship

---

80. On God enjoying diversity, see Elaine Padilla, *Divine Enjoyment: A Theology of Passion and Exuberance* (New York: Fordham University Press, 2015).

81. The idea God cannot control overcomes J. L. Schellenberg's worries about divine hiddenness. For Schellenberg's arguments, see *Divine Hiddenness and Human Reason* (Ithaca, NY: Cornell University Press, 2006); *The Hiddenness Argument* (Oxford: Oxford University Press, 2015).

God as all-powerful and then regard oppressive leaders and their policies as divinely willed. They're following the logic of omnipotence, because a God with unlimited power either wants or allows all political leaders and policies.

It's time to end omnipotence. Fortunately, killing it does not mean killing God. If we detach the traditional answers to evil from the idea that God has unlimited power, we can salvage most of them. The God who emerges better fits scripture, philosophy, and everyday experience. And we can resolve a host of troubling issues that lead many to doubt a loving God exists.

The death of omnipotence brings plausibility to belief. God makes more sense. But the entombing of omnipotence also raises questions. Perhaps the chief is this: "What does a nonomnipotent God *do?*"

I turn to address that question.

4

Amipotence

If omnipotence is dead, how should we talk about God's power? What does God *do*? And how does God do it?

In *God and the Problem of Evil*, William Hasker asks me this question. "Given the limitations imposed by [Oord's view], what *can* God do about what goes on in the world?"[1] When asking, Hasker knew only a portion of my writing. But the question arose for many who read my books, *God Can't* and *The Uncontrolling Love of God.*[2]

We need a plausible account of who God is and what God does.

It's hard to exaggerate the benefits of saying God is not omnipotent. A God who cannot control creatures or circumstances is not morally

---

1. Hasker is responding to the short essay I wrote for a five views book. See William Hasker, "The Open Theist Response," in *God and the Problem of Evil*, 162. Richard Rice explores problems with saying God is limited in *The Future of Open Theism: Antecedents and Opportunities* (Downers Grove, Ill.: IVP Academic, 2020). See my review of Rice's book and the topic of limits in "Open Theism and Divine Limitations" http://thomasjayoord. com/index.php/blog/archives/open-theism-and-the-question-of-divine-limitations (Accessed 12/6/21).

2. I have since outlined my view of divine action in several writings. See, for instance, *Questions and Answers for God Can't*, chapter 5, *Open and Relational Theology*, chapter 6, and *Pluriform Love*, chapters 7-8.

responsible for failing to prevent evil. Victims and survivors send notes thanking me for explaining this view, which says God loves everyone and everything but can't control anyone or anything. This theology changes lives for good.

Most people do not know, however, the mistranslations and mistaken interpretations of scripture that led to God being called "omnipotent." And most don't realize the countless philosophical qualifications it requires. Consequently, many think omnipotence is a live option. It's not.

When the problems of divine sovereignty are pointed out, some people assume they have to choose between omnipotence or impotence, a God who does everything or a God who does nothing. I don't find either option appealing . . . or plausible.

Fortunately, there's a better way to think. In this chapter, I introduce amipotence. With the death of omnipotence, we need a robust alternative to explain what God does, a view that fits our experience, reason, and scripture. Something better is born to displace the dead.

Amipotence replaces omnipotence.

Amipotence

Amipotence combines two Latin words *ami* and *potens*. The first means "love," and we find it in words like "amicable," "amity," and "amigo." The second is the Latin word for power or influence, and we find it in "potential" and "potency." Amipotence is pronounced "am" (as in "Amsterdam"), with a short "i" (as in "it"), and "po-tence" (similar to "moments").

Am-i-po-tence.

I coined this word to stress the priority of love over power in God.[3] Divine love (*ami*) comes logically and conceptually prior to divine power

---

3. Bradford McCall argues for something similar with "amorepotent." See *The God of Chance & Purpose: Divine Involvement in a Secular Evolutionary World* (Eugene, Or.: Wipf

(*potens*). Amipotence presumes that we best understand God in general, and divine power in particular, if we give love pride of place. Divine love preconditions and governs divine power. Love comes first.

Amipotence interprets the Johannine phrase "God is love" (1 Jn. 4:8,16) to mean we should begin with love when trying to understand who God is and what God does. We would be wise to believe God is necessarily loving, because it's God's eternal and unchanging nature to love. God could no more stop loving than stop existing, but both are metaphysical impossibilities. Amipotence agrees with John Wesley when he says, "God is often styled holy, righteous, wise . . . [but] he is said to *be* love: intimating that this is . . . his reigning attribute, the attribute that sheds an amiable glory on all his other perfections."[4]

Crucial to making sense of amipotence is making sense of love. Most theologians say God loves, and some say divine love is powerful. But few define love carefully or allow love to characterize divine power in a satisfactory way. As a result, the majority portray God's love as *radically* different from what we consider love.

Love as we know it involves giving and receiving relationships, for instance, but theologians like Augustine and David Bentley Hart say God's love is nonrelational or impassible.[5] Love as we know it is expressed moment by moment, but theologians like Thomas Aquinas and Paul Helm say God's love is timeless.[6] While our love often, if not always, includes emotion, theologians like Anselm and James Dolezal say divine love

& Stock, 2021). Roger Wolsey argues compellingly for "omniamo" in *Kissing Fish* (Roger Wolsey, 2011).

4. John Wesley, *Explanatory Notes on the New Testament* (New York: Lanes and Scott, 1850), 1 John 4:8. For a scholarly overview of Wesley's theology, see Randy L. Maddox, *Responsible Grace* (Nashville, Tenn.: Kingswood, 1994).

5. For Hart's view, see *The Hidden and the Manifest* (Grand Rapids, Mich.: Eerdmans, 2017).

6. For Helm's view, see *Eternal God* (Oxford: Oxford University Press, 1988).

includes no emotional response to creatures.[7] And although love prevents evil that is preventable, theologians like Jacob Arminius and Jack Cottrell say a loving God could prevent harm, horrors, and holocausts but chooses not to do so.[8]

We best define the love in amipotence as acting intentionally, in relational response to God and others, to promote overall well-being. This definition applies to both divine and creaturely love. The love God and creatures express, in other words, acts with intention, relates with others, and aims to promote flourishing.[9] And because love is inherently uncontrolling, neither divine nor creaturely love controls.[10]

Love can't be omnipotent.

While the definition of love applies to God and creatures, God's love is greater in degree. Divine love is universal and therefore differs in scope because only God is omnipresent. God's love differs in duration and frequency because God loves everlastingly. Divine love differs in adequacy because God is omniscient and better knows what promotes well-being.[11] Divine love is necessary because it's God's nature to love; creatures may or may not love.[12] Divine love is perfectly sensitive and vulnerable because God is affected by all creation. Creatures often fail to empathize.

---

7. For Dolezal's view, see *All that Is in God* (Reformation Heritage Books, 2017).

8. For Cottrell's view, see "The Nature of Divine Sovereignty," in *The Grace of God, the Will of Man*.

9. I explain this definition in *Defining Love: A Philosophical, Scientific, and Theological Engagement* (Grand Rapids, Mich.: Brazos, 2010), chs. 1-2 and *Pluriform Love*, ch. 2. Stephen G. Post has written often and well on love. Among his many books, see *Unlimited Love* (Philadelphia: Templeton, 2003).

10. For explorations of uncontrolling love from therapists, psychologists, and counselors, see *Love Does Not Control* Annie L. DeRolf, et. al., eds. (Grasmere, Id.: SacraSage, 2023).

11. As an open and relational theologian, I believe God knows all that's knowable. What's knowable includes what has occurred in the past, is occurring in the present, is possible for the future, and all forms/eternal objects. But even a person who endorses a classic view of omniscience should agree with my claim about the adequacy of omniscience for love.

12. Ilia Delio writes powerfully about God's nature of love in *The Emergent Christ* (Maryknoll, N.Y.: Orbis, 2012).

The "potence" of amipotence pertains to God's influence. Divine power is immensely more influential than creaturely power. God is more powerful, in part, because an omnipresent God affects all creation. God's love is more powerful because it is everlastingly relentless; it never ends. The power of amipotence is active and receptive, empowering and empathetic, wooing but persistent, and always uncontrolling. Divine love is literally the most powerful force in the universe.

An amipotent God is not omnipotent in the sense of having all power. It is impossible for a loving God to have all power, because love requires others with power. An amipotent God is not omnipotent in the sense of being able to do absolutely anything. Love cannot sin, cannot force its own way, cannot be isolated, cannot determine outcomes singlehandedly, cannot make 2 + 2 = 7, and more. And an amipotent God does not control creatures or circumstances, because love is inherently uncontrolling. God exerts maximal power but—thank goodness—is not omnipotent.

Amipotence is maximal divine power in the service of love.

The Priority of Love

I'm not the first to say God's love is powerful. Some theologians propose labels like "omnipotent love," "love almighty," "sovereign love," or "all-powerful love."[13] Most who coin such labels, however, retain one of the

---

13. Those who refer to God's power as "omnipotent love" or something similar include Gustaf Aulen, *The Faith of the Christian Church* (Eugene, Or.: Wipf and Stock, 2003 [1960]); Leonardo Boff, *Church: Charism and Power*, John W. Diercksmeier, trans. (New York: Crossroad, 1986); Vincent Brümmer, *The Model of Love: A Study in Philosophical Theology* (New York: Cambridge Univ. Press, 1993); Ilia Delio, *The Unbearable Wholeness of Being: God, Evolution, and the Power of Love* (Maryknoll, N.Y.: Orbis, 2013); Austin Farrer, *Love Almighty and Ills Unlimited* (Garden City, N.Y.: Doubleday, 1961); Nels F. S. Ferré, *The Christian Understanding of God* (New York: Harper, 1951); Søren Kierkegaard, *Søren Kierkegaard's Journals and Papers*, Vol. 2, Howard V. Hong and Edna H. Hong, ed. and trans. (Bloomington, Ind.: Indiana University Press, 1967–1978); Bradford McCall, *The God of Chance & Purpose*; Daniel Migliore, *The Power of God and the Gods of Power* (Louisville, Ky.: John Knox, 2008); George M. Newlands, *God in Christian Perspective* (Edinburgh: T&T Clark, 1994); LeRon Shults, *Reforming the Doctrine of God* (Grand Rapids, Mich.:

three primary meanings of omnipotence. They add "love" to assure believers that divine sovereignty, as they conceive it, is not brute force, sheer control, or arbitrary rule. They wrongly think God can be simultaneously all-loving and all-powerful.

In his best-selling book, *Crazy Love*, Francis Chan advocates what he calls "all-powerful love." Because he thinks the omnipotent One is self-oriented, however, Chan insists God *most* wants to be worshipped and feared. Chan says the answer to questions like "Why are so many people dying of starvation?" and "Why is my family messed up?" is "simply this: because He's God." In fact, God regards "all the peoples of the earth . . . as nothing."[14] I don't call those good answers or expressions of divine love!

Or take Hans Urs Von Balthasar's *Credo: Meditations on the Apostles' Creed*. When he explores the creed's use of "Almighty," Von Balthasar appeals to "love-almightiness." He claims the Father is "equally loving and equally powerful." We see the "unimaginable power of the Father in the force of his self-surrender," Von Balthasar says, "not in his being able to do this or that as he chooses."

The Father bestows freedom on the Son and the Spirit. What's the aim of this surrender of power? It's *not* the good of the world, according to Von Balthasar, at least not primarily. It's God's own self-love and glory. Divine love in Trinity is "complete in itself," says Von Balthasar; God "is love, responding beloved, and union of the fruit of both." Consequently, God "has need of no extradivine world in order to have something to love." If God chooses to create, the Father creates to "glorify the beloved Son." In fact, "the work of the Son and the Spirit in the world is aimed at bringing

---

Eerdmans, 2005); Kathryn Tanner, "The Power of Love," in *Renegotiating Power, Theology, and Politics*, J. Daniel and R. Elgendy, eds. (New York: Palgrave Macmillan, 2015); Hans Urs Von Balthasar, *Credo* (San Francisco: Ignatius, 1989). Paul Sponheim explores Soren Kierkegaard's view of omnipotent love in *Love's Availing Power* (Minneapolis: Fortress, 2011). David Polk offers an outstanding discussion of this issue in *God of Empowering Love*.

14. Francis Chan, *Crazy Love: Overwhelmed by a Relentless God,* rev. ed. (Colorado Springs, Colo.: David C. Cook, 2013), 30, 35-36.

all things home to this ultimate Origin."[15] Love for creation is God's afterthought, according to Von Balthasar. God necessarily self-loves; God may or may not love creatures.[16]

Chan, Von Balthasar, and most theologians who coin phrases like "omnipotent love" fail to put love first. In fact, many theologians say no divine attribute should be given priority, wanting to maintain equity among them. As Von Balthasar puts it, God is "equally loving and equally powerful."

This seems laudable. But in reality, *every* coherent theology privileges one or more divine attribute above others. Although many theologians try to give equal weight to each attribute, the discerning reader detects one as primary. One attribute functions in ways that require the others to be understood in light of it. And, usually, that attribute is omnipotence.

Let me illustrate. Many theologians talk about God's omnipotent freedom to do whatever God decides. They say God can love creation, for instance, or not love it. God could have chosen not to create and remain everlastingly in solitude, and a sovereign God can freely withdraw from creation. These claims privilege God's omnipotent freedom *from* creation above God's love *for* it.[17] In them, power comes before love.

Eberhard Jüngel identifies the problem. When God is understood as "the almighty Lord," says Jüngel, "love and mercy appear to be fundamentally secondary and subsidiary to his claim to lordship. This is the earthly

---

15. Hans Urs Von Balthasar, *Credo: Meditations on the Apostle's Creed,* David Kipp, trans. (San Francisco: Ignatius, 1990), 31-32.

16. Amipotence is not opposed to intra-trinitarian love. There's no reason God can't everlastingly love in Trinity and everlastingly love creatures. But amipotence doesn't *require* belief in the Trinity. Muslims, Jews, and Unitarians, for instance, can affirm amipotence. For more on the advantages and disadvantages of affirming the Trinity, see Karen Baker-Fletcher, *Dancing with God* (Chalice, 2006); Joseph Bracken: *God: Three Who Are One* (Liturgical, 2017); Dale Tuggy, *What is the Trinity?* (Createspace, 2017); Keith Ward, *Christ and Cosmos* (Cambridge, 2015).

17. Migliore titles one of his chapters, "The Power of God Who Freely Loves." See his book, *The Power of God and the gods of Power.*

way of thinking of a lord: first he has all power and then perhaps he can be merciful—but then again, perhaps not. God's lordliness and lordship are thought of in the same general way. He is mighty, able, and free to love or not to love . . . the love of God becomes a secondary attribute."[18]

In amipotence, by contrast, divine love comes logically prior to sovereign choice. Consequently, God *has* to love creatures and creation; it's God's eternal nature to do so. When love comes first, God cannot choose *not* to love. And when love for creation is an eternal and essential attribute, God everlastingly loves creatures. It's a metaphysical impossibility that God would love in absolute isolation; the Maker always makes love recipients. To use a sex analogy, God always makes love with creatures, and something new is conceived in these encounters.

Saying God *has* to love does not mean God is altogether without freedom. Open and relational theologians like me believe God loves moment by moment, facing an open, yet-to-be-determined future. Consequently, God freely chooses *how* to love in each moment, given the possibilities and circumstances. Because God cannot be certain how free creatures will respond, God freely selects among the best options and calls creatures to choose.[19] By nature, God *must* love, but in experience, God *freely* chooses how to love. These are features of God's essence-experience binate.[20]

Theologies that start with God's self-sufficient omnipotence ask *whether* God will create. According to them, God could remain eternally

---

18. Eberhard Jüngel, *God as the Mystery of the World*, tr. Darrell L. Guder (Grand Rapids: Eerdmans, 1983), 21. Paul Sponheim reimagines divine power in light of love in *Love's Availing Power* and Brian Zahnd aims to rethink God in light of love in *Sinners in the Hands of a Loving God* (London: Waterbrook, 2017).

19. This idea overcomes William L. Rowe's worry that a perfectly loving God cannot be free. An open and relational God cannot foreknow with certainty what creatures will freely choose, so God freely chooses among best options in each moment. See Rowe's argument in *Can God Be Free?* (Oxford: Oxford University Press, 2004).

20. I have explained God's essence-experience binate in previous books. For instance, see *The Uncontrolling Love of God*, ch. 7 and *Pluriform Love*, ch. 4.

alone, engaged in self-love but never creating or loving creaturely others.[21] Amipotence theologies, by contrast, start with God's love for creatures and creation. In them, God necessarily and everlastingly creates others to love.

Theologies in which omnipotence takes precedence ask *whether* God will give power, agency, and freedom to creatures. An all-powerful God could exert all power. By contrast, amipotence assumes that divine love always and necessarily provides power to creatures. Because love comes first, amipotence gives and respects the "otherness" of creaturely others.

Theologies in which omnipotence predominates ponder *whether* God will choose to control creatures from time to time, occasionally overriding or withholding power. According to them, God is voluntarily self-limited. The love of amipotence, by contrast, is inherently uncontrolling. An amipotent God cannot singlehandedly determine outcomes. Amipotence can't control.

When conceptual tensions arise among divine attributes, amipotence reconfigures the others to suit what love requires. It does not claim love is God's *only* attribute. Amipotence doesn't dismiss omnipresence, omniscience, everlastingness, wisdom, covenantal faithfulness, divine power, and so on. But it looks at each through the lens of love. The result means God's attributes are configured differently than how most theologies configure them. Love prevails.[22]

The amipotent God is affected by creatures, for instance, and experiences emotions: God feels. The omniscience of amipotence involves God

---

21. Amipotence theologies are neutral on the question of intratrinitarian love. Social trinitarians attracted to the intratrinitarian love proposal can accept amipotence, because there's no contradiction between God everlastingly loving within Trinity and everlastingly loving creatures. But those who reject the Trinity should also find amipotence amenable.

22. Amipotence agrees with Martin Luther King, Jr. when he says, "Power without love is reckless and abusive, and love without power is sentimental and anemic." It agrees with King that "Power at its best is love implementing the demands of justice, and justice at its best is power correcting everything that stands against love." Amipotence adds that in God, love enjoys conceptual primacy. Although powerful, God cannot overpower when implementing justice.

receiving new information moment by moment, not foreknowing from all eternity: God timefully perceives. An amipotent God creates alongside creatures and creation rather than overpowering or conjuring something from nothing: God co-creates. The steadfast love of an amipotent God is relentless; divine love for creation literally endures forever. An amipotent Lover forgives and never sends anyone to hell: God redeems. An amipotent God enjoys covenantal relations—*hesed*—with all creation: God relates. Divine wisdom rests primarily upon compassion for all rather than self-referential glory: God cares.

The logical priority of love makes a difference in how we think about God.

God Acts Somewhat Like Creatures Act

The foregoing provides my basic answer to the question, "What does God do?" But this answer remains somewhat vague. I want to address more specifically how an amipotent God acts. I begin, however, by comparing my view with others.

Amipotence disagrees with theologians who answer the question, "What does God do?" with "God does *everything*." That answer assumes the implausible view that God is all-determining. Omnipotence theologies say God could or does exert all power. But amipotence is not omnipotence.

Amipotence also disagrees with those who answer the question, "God does *nothing*."[23] Those theologies align better with deism, with God watching creation from afar. It makes no sense to say an amipotent God has maximal power—as I do—but claim God does nothing. Amipotence is not impotence.

The more common response to "What does God do?" is no answer at all. In explicit or subtle ways, many theologians appeal to mystery. Because

---

23. For an example of a contemporary deist, see Michael A. Corey, *Back to Darwin: The Scientific Case for Deistic Evolution* (Lanham, Md.: University Press of America, 1994), 15.

God is utterly incomprehensible, they say, we know *nothing* about what God does. God is hidden, inscrutable, or unknowable.

Representing Augustine and Aquinas, Michael J. Dodds advocates this approach.[24] "We should be cautious about trying to say anything about how God acts," says Dodds. "God is totally other."[25] For this reason, "the mode or manner of divine activity will ever escape us."[26] After all, "God's action is fundamentally different from that of creatures."[27] According to Dodds, we can't answer the question, "What does God do?" in a constructive way.[28]

Amipotence assumes God's acting is like creaturely acting, at least in some ways. The basic meaning of "act" applies to God and creatures, for instance, as well as the basic meanings of "relate," "experience," and "love."

---

24. Augustine uses the philosophical category of "accidents" to talk about divine action. Accidental properties "can be either lost or diminished," he explains, and they exist "in relation to something." He gives the following list of accidents: "friendships, relationships, services, likenesses, equalities, and anything else of the kind." They also include "places and times, acts and passions" (Augustine, *Trinity* V:17). But, says Augustine, "in God, *nothing* is said to be according to accident." This means God can't act, relate, be a friend, experience time, or be like creatures in any way. Of course, Augustine talks in various writings about God creating, revealing, saving, and so on. But those claims don't fit his philosophical commitments. He's inconsistent. The best one can say is that Augustine's God mysteriously *does* things in a nonacting, timeless, unresponsive, nonexperiential way. And that's *nothing* like what we know as "doing" things or acting. For my full criticism of Augustine, see *Pluriform Love*, chs. 5-6.

25. Michael J. Dodds, O.P., *Unlocking Divine Action: Contemporary Science and Thomas Aquinas* (Catholic University of America, 2017), 161. For my review of Dodds's book, see "Unlocking Divine Action," *Christian Scholar's Review* 43:2 (Winter 2013), 191-94.

26. Dodds, *Unlocking Divine Action*, 169.

27. Ibid., 171. Thomas Aquinas claims God is a primary cause working through secondary causes of creation. But if we ask what the primary cause *does*, we get answers that have nothing in common with what we know as "doing." Dodds explains: "These causes do not belong to the same order" (191). This means that "when a primary and secondary cause act together, the effect belongs entirely to both" (192). In other words, this is a version of compatibilism, with all the incoherence that comes from saying God entirely causes something and creatures also cause it. Dodds admits the proposal leads to incomprehensibility: "We must hold firmly to two apparently contradictory truths. God does whatever creatures do; and that creatures themselves do whatever they do" (208). Compatibilism is inconceivable; we should reject versions of primary-secondary causation that assume it.

28. So called "negative theology" aligns with the tradition of Aquinas and others. Rather than answering the question, "What does God do?" negative theology tell us what God cannot do.

God is not an exception to the ontological principles of existence.[29] Divine action is not entirely mysterious.

To use Aristotelean categories, an amipotent God acts as an efficient cause. God is part of the causal network of existence as one cause among others, albeit present to all others. God influences creatures in ways similar to how creatures influence. God relates, experiences, and loves likes creatures, and in these ways, God's doing is analogous to ours.

Differences between Creator and creation remain, of course. Amipotence does not consider God in all ways identical to creatures. God is transcendent and immanent: different from creatures in some ways, but like them in others. Without similarities, we cannot make constructive claims about what God does. Without differences, we cannot distinguish Creator from creatures.

The Spirit Interacts with Creation

I agree with those who say God is a universal but invisible spirit without a localized body. God is "spirit," says Jesus (Jn. 4:24), and "No one has ever seen God," says John (1:18; 4:12). The divine Spirit is bodiless or "incorporeal," say most theologians. And God is omnipresent or universal (Ps. 139), in the sense of being immediately present to every creature and all creation.

Exploring God's action as a universal, invisible, and incorporeal Spirit helps us answer questions about what it means for God to do something. If God is Spirit, for instance, the divine ontology is spiritual. Writers of scripture and theologians across the ages use words like "breath," "mind," "wind," and "soul" to account for the divine ontological makeup. God is *ruach*, to quote Hebrew writers, and *pneuma*, to quote the New Testament. Both words describe the divine ontology, God's spiritual composition.

---

29. I agree with Alfred North Whitehead on this point. See *Process and Reality*, 521.

Understanding God as the "universal mind" or "the soul of the universe" points to several truths. Minds are intentional, for instance, and a loving God acts intentionally. Minds interact with brains and bodies, influencing them and being influenced. A loving God is analogously relational, although God interacts with all creation.[30] Minds perceive and know. The loving Spirit is all-perceptive and all-knowing, which is essential to fulfill God's aim to promote overall well-being.

When translated "breath" and "wind," *ruach* and *pneuma* connote life and causation. God's metaphorical breathing into Adam depicts the divine Spirit enlivening creation, for instance (Gen. 2:7). God is the source of life. Jesus refers to the spirit "that blows where it wishes" (Jn. 3:8), which suggests God's loving causation makes a difference but cannot be tamed. A creature's breath and nature's winds are localized, of course, so adding "universal" to the "loving Spirit" reminds us that divine love is not limited to some creatures or some places.

One problem with saying God is Spirit, however, is that it leads many to distinguish sharply between a spiritual God and a material world. In this dualism, humans include both dimensions: they have material bodies but spiritual minds/souls. The conceptual conundrums this dualism generates are numerous, and exploring them all is beyond our scope. One question is pertinent, however: "How does a purely spiritual God interact with purely material creation?"[31]

One resolution to problem dismisses the spiritual altogether. According to this view, only matter is real. The resulting materialism usually dismisses God too, or it redefines deity in ways that make little sense. Reductive

---

30. For helpful books on divine action and the God-world relationship, see Joseph Bracken, *Reciprocal Causality in an Event-Filled World* (London: Lexington, 2022); Philip Clayton, *Adventures in Spirit* (Minneapolis: Fortress, 2008); John B. Cobb, Jr., *God and the World* (Philadelphia: Westminster, 1965); Nancy R. Howell, *A Feminist Cosmology* (Humanities Press, 2000).

31. Charles Taliaferro raises this important question in *A Contemporary Philosophy of Religion*, 78. I answer it with my material-mental monism framework.

materialism eliminates human mentality, decision-making, and freedom.[32] It's hard to imagine a material world having ultimate value if there is no divine Mind or creaturely minds to appreciate it.[33]

Another way to resolve the spiritual/material dualism dismisses the material world. In this approach, materiality is either an illusion or ultimately insignificant. Only minds, spirits, and ideas count and are real.[34] Some forms of idealism say only the mental matters. For those who dismiss the physical world, matter doesn't matter.

I suggest an alternative way to talk about the Spirit and creatures. It overcomes conundrums created when we accept a spiritual/material dualism to describe God and creation. This alternative draws from an ontology variously called "panpsychism," "dual-aspect monism," or "panexperientialism."[35] I call my version "material-mental monism."[36]

---

32. A group of theologians and philosophers have proposed a new version of materialism meant to overcome these concerns. See the work of Christopher Baker, Clayton Crockett, Thomas James, Adam Kotsko, and John Reader.

33. Keith Ward has written well and often about the importance of values for philosophy and theology. Among his books, see *Morality, Autonomy, and God* (London: One World, 2013). See also Andrew M. Davis, *Mind, Value, and Cosmos* (Lanham, Md.: Lexington, 2020).

34. For a theological defense of idealism, see *Idealism and Christianity*, Joshua Farris, et al., eds. (New York: Bloomsbury, 2017).

35. I first encountered these general ideas in the writings of Alfred North Whitehead, especially *Process and Reality: An Essay in Cosmology*, corrected edition, ed. David Ray Griffin and Donald W. Sherburne (New York: Free, 1978; orig. ed., 1929). John Polkinghorne calls this view "dual-aspect monism." See *Faith, Science and Understanding* (SPCK/Yale University Press, 2000), pp. 95–9. David Ray Griffin coined the word "panexperientialism" to describe this idea. See "Some Whiteheadian Comments," in *Mind in Nature: Essays on the Interface of Science and Philosophy*, eds. John B. Cobb, Jr., and David Ray Griffin (Washington, DC: University Press of America, 1977). One of the better introductions to panpsychism is from Philip Goff, *Galileo's Error* (New York: Vintage, 2020). On the fruitfulness of panpsychism for theology, see Godehard Brüntrup, et. al., eds., *Panentheism and Panpsychism: Philosophy of Religion Meets Philosophy of Mind*, (Mentis Verlag/Brill, 2020) and Joanna Leidenhag, *Minding Creation: Theological Panpsychism and the Doctrine of Creation* (London: T & T Clark, 2021).

36. Wm. Andrew Schwartz and I explain this in "Panentheism and Panexperientialism for Open and Relational Theology," in *Panentheism and Panpsychism: Philosophy of Religion Meets Philosophy of Mind*, Godehard Brüntrup, et al., eds., (Mentis Verlag/Brill, 2020). I

Material-mental monism proposes that everything that exists has both material and mental dimensions. Minds, brains, bodies, and all creation are—or are comprised of—entities with both materiality and mentality. Some creaturely objects are organized as aggregates, like rocks, water, tables, and computers. Other creatures are coordinated actors and organisms, like cells, fungi, worms, parakeets, and humans. Some actors are hybrids, with organismic and aggregate aspects, like plants and cyborgs. No matter how organized, all that exists—top to bottom, simple to complex, animate to inanimate—has material and mental aspects.

I mention this to set up a proposal: we would be wise to believe the universal, incorporeal, and invisible Spirit has material and mental dimensions. Although spiritual in the sense of being wind-like and mind-like, the divine Spirit has both materiality and mentality. The universal Holy Ghost acts like an invisible breath or undetectable intelligence in relation to all creation. That unseen presence gives and receives as a personal Spirit with both objective and subjective aspects. God, too, has material and mental facets.

If it seems farfetched to think an invisible Spirit has a material dimension, let's think a bit about air. Is air material? At first, we might say "no." But if air is primarily nitrogen and oxygen, and those are material elements, we'd have to say air is material after all. We can't touch, taste, see, smell, or hear it, however, at least not in most cases. Analogously, the divine Spirit has a material dimension we cannot touch, taste, see, smell, or hear. And this Spirit has mental capabilities similar to an invisible mind.

This proposal is not speculation for speculation's sake. It helps answer our questions "What does God do?" and "How does God do it?" If the universal Spirit of love has material and mental aspects and if creatures and creation have material and mental aspects, we can make conceptual sense of

---

prefer material-mental monism to "panpsychism" because the latter doesn't identify matter. I prefer it to "panexperientialism" because that word identifies neither mentality nor materiality. I prefer material-mental monism to "dual-aspect" monism for the same reason.

God's interaction with us. Although there are differences between God and creatures, the Spirit's material-mental ontology is not different in kind from creation's. Consequently, we don't have to think that the actions, feelings, relations, and love of God are altogether different from the actions, feelings, relations, and love of creatures. We can speak sensibly about what God "does."

The universal Spirit with material and mental dimensions never controls, of course. Although exerting real influence, God is amipotent, not omnipotent. When affirming the work of a noncoercive Spirit, we embrace the words of Zechariah: "Not by might, nor by power, but by my spirit," says the Lord (4:6)

A material-mental ontology helps us discern what the material-mental Spirit does.

Detecting an Invisible Spirit

With this explanation of the Spirit's ontology, we move to how we detect divine action. Such identifying is necessary if we're to offer a plausible answer to "What does God do?" Part of this work requires comparing the Spirit's action with creaturely actions. Without distinctions, we're likely to say, "God does everything" or "God does nothing." But this exercise raises questions about how to perceive an *invisible* Spirit.

When we identify what creatures do, we typically rely upon our five senses. "I saw him kick the ball," we might say, referring to what our eyes observe. "That odor is awful!" identifies something our noses smell. "This taco is delicious," we might say, as the savory morsels roll in our tongues. We detect these activities, entities, and more through sensory perception.

We also use our senses to make inferences about what we cannot observe. By "inferences," I mean assumptions or guesses about what's going on behind or beneath what we sense. In terms of the Spirit's activity, we may assume divine action behind or beneath something we admire, respect, or esteem. More is going on than meets the eye (or other senses).

When we see a beautiful sunset, a doe licking her newborn fawn, a soldier turning the other cheek, an act of kindness for an elderly person, and more, believers often infer that the Spirit inspired each. We have reasons to surmise that a loving, good, true, and beautiful Spirit inspires but does not entirely cause everything loving, good, true, and beautiful that occurs.

Inferring the Spirit's activity is not the same as directly perceiving God, however. Guessing that the Spirit inspired some activity isn't the same as observing the Spirit doing it. We can't answer our question "What does God do" by pointing to *everything* that happens, as if God alone does it. That's the logic of omnipotence. That thinking credits God for all that's good and blames God for evil, ugliness, and sin. It regards creaturely activity as unreal.

The primary obstacle to detecting the Spirit's doings is that an invisible and incorporeal spirit cannot be perceived by our five senses. "No one has seen God," to cite scripture again. We can't literally see God walking in the garden, for instance. Our ear drums don't literally vibrate in response to sounds from divine vocal cords. We don't literally kiss God. We cannot see, taste, hear, smell, or touch the spiritual Spirit.[37]

Biblical writers sometimes use sensory language to talk about encounters with God, of course. God walked in the garden with Adam and Eve, Genesis tells us (Gen. 3). Jacob wrestled with the Lord (Gen. 32), and Moses saw God's butt (Exod. 33). Samuel heard a divine voice (1 Sam. 3), and John heard a voice from heaven saying, "This is my beloved Son. Listen to him" (Mt. 3:17). The Psalmist instructs us to "taste and see that the Lord is good" (Ps. 34:8), which might be interpreted as licking or eating God. And so on.

If God's being or composition is spiritual, these descriptions cannot be literally true. Unless God is a shapeshifter, that is. But that possibility raises

---

37. An important exploration of what it means to perceive God is found in William P. Alston's, *Perceiving God: The Epistemology of Religious Experience* (London: Cornell University Press, 1991).

numerous problems, especially pertaining to why a spiritual being who can shapeshift into a physical one doesn't prevent evil with that temporary body. (See earlier discussions on this matter.)

Consequently, I agree with the majority of theologians who say God doesn't literally have a body. God doesn't literally walk, speak, get red in the face, kiss, and so on. We can't observe an invisible Spirit pouring a cup of water for a thirsty traveler. We can't see deity carrying a banner in protest or strategizing at the local coffee shop. The universal lover is not literally the mother breastfeeding her newborn or clouds dropping needed rain on parched landscape.

Scriptures that describe God doing such activities are metaphorical not literal. While God is present to all creation and influences everything, the Spirit doesn't have a divine body to literally perform these actions. Claims about divine embodied action are metaphors.

To take claims about God's actions as metaphors, however, does not mean we cannot perceive God at all. We don't have to dismiss statements about God's activity and our experience of the Spirit as false. We can speculate that these metaphors point to an incorporeal Spirit's actions in our lives and in the world.

To make sense of perceiving God, we should embrace what some call "nonsensory perception."[38] This way of knowing provides us access to other aspects of life, like causation, values, emotions, freedom, and more. In fact, we presuppose the truth of nonsensory perception in our daily lives. Our living requires their reality.[39]

---

38. For details on the nonsensory perception of God, see David Ray Griffin, *Founders of Constructive Postmodern Philosophy: Pierce, James, Bergson, Whitehead, and Hartshorne* (Albany, N.Y.: State University of New York Press, 1993). See also John B. Cobb, Jr., *Grace and Responsibility: A Wesleyan Theology for Today* (Nashville: Abingdon, 1995).

39. For more on this argument and the primacy of nonsensory perception to sensory perception, see David Ray Griffin, *Reenchantment without Supernaturalism: A Process Philosophy of Religion* (Ithaca, NY: Cornell University Press, 2001).

The theory of nonsensory perception assumes a robust empiricism, which says we rely upon experiences to know our world and God's activity. But we gain this knowledge in ways beyond what our five senses provide. In terms of perceiving God, nonsensory perception identifies the activity of what John Wesley called "spiritual senses." Nonsensory perception detects the actions of the Spirit.[40]

Although the idea of nonsensory perception may sound new, it fits the language of many who talk about encounters with God. Believers speak of detecting the divine, for instance, as a "still small voice," "intuition," a "feeling" a "holy nudge," an "inclination," one's "moral compass," a "hunch," an "inkling," "divine insight," an inaudible "call," a "light," one's "better angels," one's conscience, and more. Although not fully accurate, this language describes perception of that for which our five senses are not equipped. And it gives us direct access to the Spirit.

This helps us make sense of the Apostle John when he writes, "No one has ever seen God. If we love one another, God abides in us, and God's love is perfected in us" (1 Jn. 4:12). When saying no one has seen God, John is denying direct sensory perception of the divine, at least visual perception. But he's also saying love reveals God's active presence that affects us, because God "abides in us." "In us" might be best understood as the Spirit's loving activity affecting our experience. In other words, we experience God's love through nonsensory perception.

To sum up: we cannot perceive an invisible God with our five senses. We may infer the Spirit's activities, however, from what we observe in the

---

40. John Cobb puts it like this, "If God is present and working in us, as Wesley (and also process philosophy) affirms, there is nonsensory perception of God all the time . . . Instead of speaking of new spiritual senses, we can think of nonsensuous experience of the divine presence in our lives and awareness of its salvific effects" (Cobb, *Grace and Responsibility*, 75). I compare Wesley's view of spiritual sensations with nonsensory perception in "Grace and Social Science: Nonsensory Perception of God in a Constructive Postmodern Wesleyan Philosophy," *Jnanadeepa: Pune Journal of Religious Studies*, 5.2 (July 2002): 121-135. See also Kenny Johnston, "Perceiving Wesley: An Analytical Study of Epistemological Uses of Perception in John Wesley's Theology," *The Methodist Review* 14 (2002): 78-117.

world. And we can directly detect the Spirit's activity through nonsensory perception. Although we can never fully or accurately describe our interactions with God, our experience of the Spirit is real.

Implications of the Spirit's Universality

The Spirit's universality raises other issues to address when answering the question, "What does God do?" God's omnipresence points to an important difference between creaturely action and the Spirit's. In doing so, it provides a crucial reason to say an amipotent God has maximal power. Divine amipotence is far greater than creaturely power, because God has no equal (Is. 40). As the psalmist puts it, "Mightier than the thunder of the great waters, mightier than the breakers of the sea—the Lord on high is mighty" (Ps. 93:4).

Creaturely action is localized. The actor may dig a tunnel, mow the lawn, or fly through the air. The creaturely actor may be a whale jumping in the ocean. Puffy clouds floating overhead are elements of creation too, even if not embodied. A hurricane is a huge aggregate of creaturely actions. The pull of the moon on the sea tides is a massive body exerting influence, although we only see its effects. In creaturely cases, the actors, activity, and forces are restricted in location. No creature is universal.

The restricted nature of creaturely activity means we can differentiate some creaturely actions from others. Scientists experiment by separating subjects into groups, for instance. Those in the "treatment" group are given medicine, while those in the control group are not. The researchers gauge the medicine's influence by comparing subjects in the two groups. Through this process, scientists get an idea about what the medicine "does."

A universal and amipotent Spirit is different. God so conceived is present to all creation and *always* lovingly influences everyone and everything. No creature, no group, and no aspect of creation is uninfluenced by an always acting Spirit. We can't say, "God is acting here but not there."

Because the divine Spirit never controls, God also cannot temporarily eliminate creaturely factors to "do" something that's God's work alone. We can't say, "That was done *entirely* by God." That's the creature-denying logic of omnipotence.

Not everything we witness represents the will of the Spirit, however. Creatures choose to cooperate with amipotence or not. We perceive the harmful results when they opt for other than the best to which the Spirit calls. We make judgements about which creaturely actions align with the Spirit's call and which do not. We discern. If actions harm, hurt, and destroy what is good, we doubt the Spirit wanted them.

The Spirit's universal influence provides a key reason amipotence is maximal divine power and far superior to creaturely power. Only the universal Spirit is omnipresent, which means only the Spirit influences all creation at all times. There is no time nor location when God is not there and influencing. Because no creature exerts universal influence, the all-pervasive Spirit is immensely more influential than any creature.

Pantokrator has this right: the Spirit is all-holding, all-sustaining, and all-influencing.[41] God's got the whole world in divine (metaphorical) hands. But God is not all-powerful in the sense of omnipotent.

The effectiveness of God's immense power rests, in part, upon how creatures respond. That's the nature of relational love: the fruit of love's labor relies upon responses from the beloved. The love, truth, goodness, and beauty we witness in our lives and the universe reveal the efficacy of amipotence. As creatures cooperate with God's empowering and inspiring causal activity, we see flourishing, liberation, and abundant life. The poor are cared for, and captives set free. The immensity of amipotence is

---

41. In previous writings I have used "almighty" to describe God's uncontrolling power. I've said God is almighty, 1) in the sense of being mightier *than* any other being; 2) in the sense of exerting might *upon* all others; 3) in the sense that God is the source of might or empowerment *for* all. While I continue to think God can rightly be understood as almighty in these three ways, I now wish I had emphasized the priority of love in God. "Amipotence" better describes the power of God's love than "almighty" alone.

manifest as creatures of varying sizes, abilities, and complexities yield to the Spirit's wooing.

How different is amipotence from the usual views of God! An impotent God would watch from afar or be present without engaging. An omnipotent God would control, always or on occasion, and therefore be responsible for all that occurs, both good and evil. The amipotent God loves by empowering and inspiring, and part of the evidence for the strength of amipotence comes in positive creaturely responses.

God's everlasting influence + God's receptiveness + God's omnipresence + Creaturely cooperation = God's immense power. Amipotence is the maximal power of love.

PUTTING IT TOGETHER

The foregoing provides a set of claims to help us answer our question, "What does God do?" Those claims might be listed this way:

1. The amipotent Spirit always loves everyone and everything.
2. The amipotent Spirit acts but cannot control others.
3. The amipotent Spirit has no body but has material and mental dimensions.
4. The amipotent Spirit's activity cannot be perceived by our five senses.
5. The amipotent Spirit can be perceived through nonsensory perception.
6. The amipotent Spirit's influence can be inferred from what occurs.
7. The amipotent Spirit is present to and influencing all creation, all the time.
8. The amipotent Spirit is maximally powerful.

The first claim affirms the logical priority of love in God's nature. God's activity always aims at promoting overall well-being, and every creature, at every moment, is loved. The Spirit empowers and inspires all the loving that creatures do. In amipotence, we *all* live and move and have our being.

The second claim says God cannot singlehandedly bring about results. We can't point to something and say, "God alone did *that*." An amipotent God influences all creation but never controls any creation.

The third claim provides an ontological basis for understanding how God acts in relation to creatures and creation. Although God does not have a localized body, God does have material and mental dimensions and exerts efficient causation upon creation. The ontological similarity between Creator and creatures accounts at least partly for how God affects creation and for how creation affects God.

The fourth claim says that we cannot know what God does using our five senses. But we can experience God directly, says the fifth claim, through nonsensory perception. The sixth claim says we can also infer the Spirit's activity based on what we witness. Although believers sometimes talk about seeing, hearing, or tasting God, these are metaphorical statements.

The seventh claim says the Spirit is omnipresent, in the sense of being present to all that exists. Because God influences all creation, however, we cannot divide into groups those creatures whom God influences from groups God does not. Even when creatures sin or do evil, the Spirit is present, although not endorsing the harm they do. God calls creatures to do what promotes overall well-being, but they may or may not cooperate.

The final claim says the Spirit's universality, which influences every creature at every moment, is the basis for God's immense power. No creature is equal to or greater than an amipotent God. But the efficacy of amipotence requires creaturely collaboration. Love involves God and creation.

These claims, taken together, help answer the question, "What does God do?"

Mighty Deeds and Rescue Failures

The foregoing helps me fulfill a promise I made in the biblical section of this book. I promised to account for God's mighty deeds and miracles in scripture, despite my denying omnipotence. I also promised to address God's *failure* to do mighty deeds, miracles, and rescuing. Addressing both seems crucial when answering our question, "What does God do?"

Amipotence agrees with the psalmist who says God is powerful: "Great is the Lord and mighty in power" (147:5). The universal, loving Spirit inspires and empowers everything we perceive that is loving, good, true, and beautiful. God calls creatures to act in ways that promote overall well-being. Without the empowering Spirit, creatures could not do anything.

Whatever is good in the world, therefore, emerges because of the activity of the Spirit *and* creaturely responses. Loving, good, true, and beautiful events are never the products of God alone. But neither do they derive from creatures alone. Whatever is excellent and worthy of praise has God as its source and creatures as contributors.

Whatever is sinful, evil, and promotes ill-being derives from the failure of creatures or creation to cooperate with God. Because God always loves everyone and everything and God's love is empowering, God gives the abilities to creatures to do good and evil. But an amipotent God neither causes nor permits evil, as if God could disempower those God already empowered.

Denying that God is all-powerful also helps us understand why the Spirit cannot singlehandedly rescue the hurting and harmed. God *always* works for good, but creatures and creation can frustrate God's efforts. Creatures may not cooperate. The inanimate conditions of creation may not be conducive for good. Entities of various complexities may not respond well to Love's wooing. Societies or environments may not be aligned for the loving consequences God desires.[42]

---

42. For books addressing the climate crisis and living well with creation, see Philip Clayton and Wm Andrew Schwartz, *What is Ecological Civilization?* (Process Century, 2019); Jay

This helps us understand why Israel was not always rescued, for instance. God can't rescue singlehandedly. Discarding omnipotence also makes it possible to solve the problem of selective miracles. We can make sense of all the miracles *not* done by Jesus, for instance. Furthermore, the God without a localized body cannot stop evils that you, others, and I sometimes can stop with our bodies.

When God is considered amipotent, the mighty deeds in scripture and those we witness today are rightly credited to God's initiative. Thanks be to God! But they also come from cooperating creatures or conducive conditions in creation. Thanks to creation too! A humble God shares the credit.

When we witness miracles and mighty acts, God acted, and creatures responded well. Or the inanimate conditions of creation were conducive to God's working. Or smaller entities and organisms responded well to the Spirit's activity. Or creaturely environments and societies were aligned for the good God wanted. In other words, we rightly interpret all positive events as the result of God's initiating and creaturely responses or conducive conditions.

God initially created and continues to create the heavens and the earth through amipotence. God acts creatively and creation responds. The miracles in scripture and those occurring today derive from amipotence. They are evidence of God's loving power working with and alongside creatures and creation for unexpectedly good outcomes.

All things considered, therefore, amipotence makes better sense of both God's mighty acts and God's failures to rescue recorded in scripture and evident today.

McDaniel, *With Roots and Wings* (Wipf and Stock, 2009); Randy Woodley, *Shalom and the Community of Creation* (Eerdmans, 2012).

The Synergy of Amipotence

Let me say in a negative way what I have said positively. Biblical writers never explicitly say God acted alone to bring about the mighty deeds in salvation history. I know of no event recorded in scripture, nothing I have witnessed, no event others have reported, and nothing in the history of this universe that requires us to think God *alone* caused it. None. Ever.

There is no evidence for omnipotence.

Every event in scripture explicitly identifies creatures and creaturely causes at play. Or scripture allows for them, as I pointed out in the biblical chapter. Every event—from the creation of our universe to every miracle to the resurrection of Jesus and more—includes some creaturely influence, actor, factor, or force. All of them.

I'm making this claim despite not having witnessed every event, of course. I don't even know every cause of *any* event today. My knowledge is limited. But given no explicit biblical claim for unilateral determination—omnipotence—and no event outside scripture devoid of creaturely factors, actors, and forces, I speculate that every event requires both God's acting and creaturely response or conditions.

Those who claim that an omnipotent God does mighty deeds or miracles *also* haven't witnessed every event. They *also* don't know all factors and forces in any event. They have limited knowledge like I do. But believers in omnipotence face the fact that every event within scripture and outside it can be conceived as involving creaturely factors and actors. Additionally, they cannot overcome the problem of evil and the other problems I've mentioned that rightly lead people to doubt God exists. While none of us can be certain about our views of God's power, amipotence makes better sense of scripture, history, and our experience.[43]

---

43. As I said in the scripture chapter, I'm *not* saying every biblical passage portrays God as loving. While many passages do, many do not. The overall drift of scripture is best understood as pointing to a God of perfect love. The revelation of God in Jesus also suggests this.

I admit, however, that amipotence will be hard for some to grasp. The legacy of omnipotence dies hard. So many have assumed God is all-powerful when interpreting the Bible or making sense of life. Given this reality, I want to expand on the synergy logic at the heart of amipotence.

It's not hard to imagine that human salvation requires cooperation with the Spirit. At least it's not hard for those who embrace free will theologies. We have an essential role to play in the symbiotic saga of salvation. But it's difficult even for freewill theologians to imagine how the synergy of amipotence applies to lesser creatures and inanimate creation. It will be difficult for some to imagine an amipotent God creating the world, being the source of miracles, resurrecting Jesus, or fulfilling love's aim at the eschaton.

Two beliefs prevent many people from imagining God synergistically at work with all creation, from quarks to quasars. One has been the focus of this book: many assume God is omnipotent. They think God's power play is absolute overpowering. I hope the preceding pages convince readers this belief is both mistaken and destructive. It's not supported by Hebrew scriptures or the New Testament. It's the cause of countless philosophical qualifications. It leads many to reject belief in God altogether. And so on. I'll not repeat the reasons we should stop thinking God exerts all power, can do absolutely anything, or controls creatures or circumstances.

The second belief preventing people from imagining God's work as synergistic is less often identified. This belief says God gives freedom to and respects the agency *only* of humans and complex creatures. God controls everything else. It assumes simpler creatures and the basic elements of existence are dead matter, devoid of agency, and without autonomous integrity. According to this belief, God does not work synergistically with worms, cells, and atoms.

I address this issue in greater detail in *Pluriform Love*. On Jesus revealing God, see Brad Jersak, *A More Christlike God* (Plain Truth, 2016).

The idea that simpler entities have no agency or self-causation emerged among leading thinkers in the modern period. These scholars imagined the universe to be machine-like, with creaturely parts operating like mindless cogs. Rather than being alive, the universe and its creatures were thought to be experientially dead, like grains of sand rather than pulsing organisms.

Fortunately, a growing number of people reject this mechanistic vision of existence.[44] We have reasons to believe creation is animated, spirited, alive, organismic, or enchanted.[45] The idea of an animated world fits the general biblical view too.[46] It provides reasons to think God works alongside and with even the simplest of entities and elements. The Spirit engages an enspirited creation.

If God is the giver of life and existence, we would be wise to say the Spirit provides integrity, agency, self-organization, and freedom to all creation, depending on their complexity. God gives robust freedom to complex creatures like you and me. God gives agency and self-organization to simpler creatures. And God gives the integrity of existence to the smallest entities. The Spirit gives these gifts moment by moment and cannot override or dismiss *any*. These gifts from God are, to use the language of the Apostle Paul, "irrevocable" (Rom. 11:29).

God loves quarks, for instance, and that means giving them the integrity necessary for their "quarkness." The same is true for cells, worms, sheep, and mountains. God gives the gifts of integrity, agency, and freedom

---

44. For a summary of the scientific, philosophical and theological considerations of mechanism, see John Hedley Brooke, *Science and Religion: Some Historical Perspectives* (Cambridge: Cambridge University Press, 1991), chs. 2–4. John Polkinghorne explains why the mechanistic view of existence is unhelpful. See, for instance, *The Polkinghorne Reader: Science, Faith, and the Search for Meaning*, ed. Thomas Jay Oord (West Conshohocken, PA: Templeton Press, 2010), 21-24.

45. Although many make this argument, I especially recommend Mark I. Wallace, *When God Was a Bird: Christianity, Animism, and the Re-Enchantment of the World* (New York: Fordham University Press, 2018).

46. Among scholars who make such claims, see Amos Yong, *The Spirit of Creation: Modern Science and Divine Action in the Pentecostal-Charismatic Imagination* (Grand Rapids, Mich.: Eerdmans, 2011).

to rats and cats, frogs and dogs, seeds, snakes, and civilizations. And the law-like regularities of existence emerge from God's steadfast love for all creatures and creation.[47] These gifts are evident in the material-mental monism ontology I sketched earlier.[48]

Amipotence says that life is a divine gift, but it's a gift God *necessarily* gives. An amipotent God, among whose attributes love comes first, *must* give freedom, agency, self-organization, and integrity to all creation, depending on their complexity. God cannot fail to provide, withdraw, or override the gifts given. God loves necessarily.

The Spirit gives gifts *not* because some outside force, law, or factor forces this giving. God gives gifts because love gives gifts. Because God's eternal and immutable nature is self-giving and others-empowering love, the Spirit *must* give integrity, self-organization, agency, and freedom to creatures and creation.

This drastically changes how believers think about divine power. In omnipotence, power comes logically first. Consequently, theologians who say God is all-powerful wonder why God would choose to create. Many claim God did so primarily to display sovereign glory. Those who start with omnipotence also wonder if God will decide to share power after creating. They wonder if God will control creatures or circumstances from time to time. Omnipotence theologians assume that mighty acts and miracles must be instances of God singlehandedly bringing about results. And the logic of omnipotence assumes God will someday use overriding power to make things right.

---

47. I address God's relation to so-called "natural laws" in *The Uncontrolling Love of God*. We do better to call them "law-like regularities," and they emerge because of God's omnipresence and love for all creation.

48. This is just one of many problems that material-mental monism can overcome. For a review of how the general approach of panpsychism helps, see a review of Joanna Leidenhag's book on the subject by Tim Miller and me, "Can Panpsychism Solve Thorny Theological Problems?" *Religious Studies*, (2023), 1-4.

The logic of amipotence differs dramatically. It *starts* with God loving creatures: God is love. Love was and always is God's reason for creating. Because God everlastingly loves, in fact, God everlastingly creates. In the logic of amipotence, it's never a question of *whether* God will share power. It's the nature of love to do so. The theologian of amipotence never wonders why God doesn't occasionally control others. Love, by nature, is uncontrolling. Mighty deeds and miracles are the result of God's initiation and creaturely responses or conducive conditions. Love's ultimate victory will not come through absolute control but through relentless love. Feasting at heaven's metaphorical banquet is possible through relentless amipotence, which persuades all to join the ways and power of love.

According to amipotence, the divine-creation synergy wasn't God's afterthought, backup plan, or a late evolutionary addition. The Spirit's synergy with creation is uncontrolling love at all times and all places. God necessarily gifts the elements of otherness to creatures great and small, to creation simple and highly organized, to all things now and forever.

Conclusion

I began this chapter with William Hasker's question, "What can God do?" My response is that God loves. Divine love involves real action that makes a real difference to everyone and everything. Although uncontrolling, the love of an amipotent God is literally the most powerful force in the universe.

With the demise of omnipotence, we need a replacement. I propose amipotence. It assumes uncontrolling love comes conceptually first in God's nature, logically prior to and therefore characterizing divine power. It has the advantage of solving the problem of evil, accounting for God's failures to rescue, solving the problem of selective miracles, and overcoming numerous obstacles to belief. Amipotence was the primary but not the only force at the creation of our universe and the primary but not the only force throughout evolutionary history. It's the primary cause of all that's loving, true, good, and beautiful in our personal and communal lives.

I also offered a theory for *how* God acts. That theory affirms traditional claims about God as a universal but incorporeal Spirit of love. This Spirit's actions empower and inspire creatures to love. Creatures directly perceive the Spirit's love through nonsensory perception, but they can also infer the effects of the Spirit in what they perceive with their five senses. The synergy of Creator and creation accounts for God's mighty acts in scripture and today, while attributing God's failure to rescue or stop evil to uncooperative creatures or the nonalignment of conditions in creation. The Spirit's amipotence is the greatest force in the universe.

One does not have to be a Christian to affirm amipotence.[49] Muslims and Jews can also affirm the priority of the Spirit's love and reject the absurdity of omnipotence.[50] So can theists of other religious traditions and theists who identify with no tradition at all. Although I am a Christian who tries to follow the way of Jesus, amipotence is not reserved for Christianity.

To my mind, the reasons to reject omnipotence and adopt amipotence are overwhelming. But I recognize that omnipotence has long been aligned with belief in God, and some can't imagine believing in a nonomnipotent deity. They'd rather choose atheism than think God is not all-powerful.

Atheists can love, of course. But by not believing in God, they do not embrace the positive elements that come from affirming a universal,

---

49. In this book, I have not built my argument for amipotence based upon the revelation of God found in Jesus of Nazareth. I've made that argument in other books. For instance, see *The Uncontrolling Love of God* and *Pluriform Love*. For a response to the criticism that my work fails to draw upon the Trinity, "Analogies of Love between God and Creatures: Thomas Jay Oord Responds to Kevin Vanhoozer," in *Love, Human and Divine: Contemporary Essays in Systematic and Philosophical Theology* (London: T & T Clark Publishers, 2019).

50. Among those exploring an open and relational view of God, see Bradley Shavit Artson, *God of Becoming and Relationship* (Jewish Lights, 2016); Shai Held, *Abraham Joshua Heschel* (Indiana University, 2013); John Sanders and Klaus von Stosch, eds., *Divine Action: Challenges for Muslim and Christian Theology* (Paderborn: Brill, 2022). For articles and essays from Farhan Shah, see the Open Horizons website (https://www.openhorizons.org/farhan-shah.html).

divine Lover. They do not connect their motivation to love to the Loving Mind of the universe. They do not find strength in believing a universal Spirit empowers, inspires, and accompanies them in the work of love. Or think this Suffering Spirit empathizes with them in their suffering, as a fellow sufferer who understands. Thinking we must choose between belief in an all-powerful God or in no God seems especially misguided given that scripture doesn't require omnipotence and philosophers qualify it to death.

Amipotence affirms the existence of a powerful God whose universal influence is uncontrolling love. It better fits the biblical witness and avoids the countless qualifications omnipotence requires. It overcomes the main reason many say they can't believe God exists: the problem of evil. Amipotence accounts for what's loving, true, good, and beautiful in creation without making God responsible for the evil, ugly, and bad. And it provides hope for the victory of good over evil now and in the future.

Omnipotence is dead. But amipotence can live.

ABOUT THE AUTHOR

Thomas Jay Oord, Ph.D., is a theologian, philosopher, and scholar of multidisciplinary studies. Oord directs the Center for Open and Relational Theology and doctoral students at Northwind Theological Seminary. He is an award-winning and bestselling author who has written or edited more than thirty books. A gifted speaker, Oord lectures at universities, conferences, churches, seminaries, and institutions. A world-renown theologian, Oord is also known for his research in science and religion, open and relational theology, the problem of suffering, and the implications of freedom for transformational relationships.

For more information, see Dr. Oord's website:
thomasjayoord.com

For more on the doctoral program Dr. Oord directs, see
northwindseminary.org/center-for-open-relational-theology

For more on the Center for Open and Relational Theology, see
c4ort.com

ACKNOWLEDGEMENTS

Because of my friends, this book is better than it would have been otherwise.

I am especially grateful to Brian Felushko for his help analyzing biblical references to words mistranslated "almighty." I also thank George Lyons, Richard Middleton, Karen Winslow, and Bill Yarchin for going the extra mile in their help with biblical issues. I thank Andrew Davis, Ryan Mullins, and Yugin Nagasawa for their suggestions on the philosophical chapter. I'm grateful to those endorsed the book, including Ilia Delio, Peter Enns, Catherine Keller, Ryan Mullins, Yujin Nagasawa, and Sarah Lane Ritchie.

I'm encouraged by my doctoral students at Northwind Theological Seminary. I thank them for their questions, advice, and insights. It's a joy to help each pursue big issues that matter! I also thank Seminary President Robert Duncan and Academic Dean Michael Christensen for their support.

I express my deep gratitude to the following people, many of whom also read early drafts of this book. I thank Alan Allard, Jake Baker-Brown, Fred Balliet, Chad Bahl, Cypress Brannon, Michael Brennan, Bob Brooke, Brandon Brown, David Brown, Dustin Burlet, Anna Case-Winters, Tamara Coleman, Nathan Croy, John Dally, Ulrick Rafsinger Dam, Andrew

Davis, Paul Dazet, Denver Brew Theology, Teri Ditslear, Barrett Evans, Greg Farrand, Brian Felushko, Karl Forehand, Jonathan Foster, Wendy Francisco, Rex Gray, Shai Held, Aaron Hendry, Eric Hughes, Jennifer Jensen, Bradley Jersak, David L. Jones, Mark Karris, Danny Klopovic, Sven Leisegang, John Loppnow, Alan Love, Jeff Lowe, George Lyons, Marty Michelson, Richard Middleton, Bruce Morgan, Craig Morton, Alexa Oord, Suzie Park, Josh Patterson, Phillip Poole, Austin Pounds, Janel Apps Ramsey, Stephen Riley, Michael Rose, Shawn Ryan, Kevin Sandlin, Andrew Schwartz, Pete Shaw, Jc Sheridan, Bill and Wanda Sinkey, Jill Schneider Smith, F. Scott Spencer, Melissa Owens Stewart, Richard Thompson, Brad Topp-Lowe, Maribeth Trueblood, Tracy Tucker, Don Vande Krol, Gijsbert Van Den Brink, Devon Van Essen, Sandy Wehnes, Clarence White, Karen Winslow, Deanna Young, William Yarchin, and Tamara Zaida.

INDEX

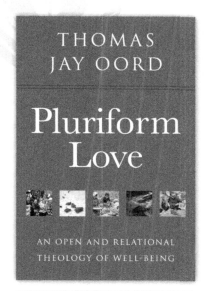

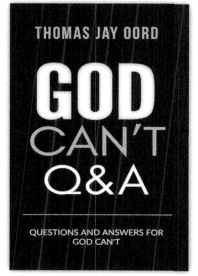
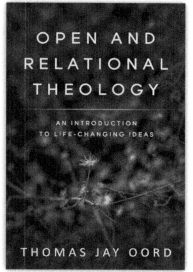

Printed in Great Britain
by Amazon